DRINK FROM THE WELL

DRINK FROM THE WELL

A guide to recognizing your fears and letting them go

ELIORA

gatekeeper press
Columbus, Ohio

The views and opinions expressed in this book are solely those of the author and do not reflect the views or opinions of Gatekeeper Press. Gatekeeper Press is not to be held responsible for and expressly disclaims responsibility of the content herein.

Drink From the Well: A guide to recognizing your fears and letting them go

Published by Gatekeeper Press
2167 Stringtown Rd, Suite 109
Columbus, OH 43123-2989
www.GatekeeperPress.com

Copyright © 2022 by Eliora
All rights reserved. Neither this book, nor any parts within it may be sold or reproduced in any form or by any electronic or mechanical means, including information storage and retrieval systems, without permission in writing from the author. The only exception is by a reviewer, who may quote short excerpts in a review.

The cover design, interior formatting, typesetting, and editorial work for this book are entirely the product of the author. Gatekeeper Press did not participate in and is not responsible for any aspect of these elements.

Library of Congress Control Number: 2021951146

ISBN (paperback): 9781662923005

Table of Contents

Preface	ix
Section 1 The Starting Place	**1**
Who Are We?	3
The Way We Change	4
The Story- Ropes	**5**
Our Relationship with Fear	7
Tools to Connect: A Meditation to Connect with Your Light	9
The Story- Two Journeys	**14**
Our Journey	17
The Story- Lessons in Belonging	**20**
Section 2 Learning to Live with Fear	**21**
Making Changes	23
Creating Expectation for Others	26
The Story- Dreams	**28**
Fear Versus Love	29
The Effects of Fear	30
Our Shared Fears	32
The Ten Foundational Fears	32
Tools to Connect: Connecting with the Light in Children	**35**
Fear and Our Suit of Darkness	37
Our Dance with Fear	41
Tools to Connect: Listening to the Quiet Voice Within	44

Section 3 Protecting Ourselves from Fear: Ours and Other People's — 49

Understanding Our Suit of Darkness — 49
These Lessons are Stored Deep in Our Subconscious — 53
Legacy Beliefs — 55
The Story- Hand-Me-Down — 56
Legacy Beliefs continued — 57
Our Societal Beliefs — 58
Our Trauma-Induced Beliefs — 60
Tools to Connect: Reliving Past Moments of Light — 62
Living Protected by Our Fear — 64
The Lens of Fear — 66
Conscious Versus Subconscious — 69

Section 4: The Patterns Created from our Subconscious Belief — 71

The Patterns of Blame — 73
The Story- The Elephant — 77
The First Pattern: Blaming-In — 79
The Second Pattern: Blaming-Out — 83
The Third Pattern: The Pretenders — 87
What Happens to These Patterns When Fear is No Longer Present? — 89
Tools to Connect: Which Blame Pattern Do You Have? — 90
Four More Patterns: "The Best of the Best," "Wallflower," "Mr. or Ms. Right," or "Fake It 'Til You Make It" — 94
The Story- Faith — 98
Pattern One: The Best of the Best — 101

The Story- Questions	**104**
Pattern Two: Wallflowers	107
The Story- Blue Lotus	**109**
Pattern Three: Mr. or Ms. Right	111
The Story- To Connect to the Divine: Choose One of the Best Memories of Your Life	**113**
Pattern Four: "Fake It 'Til You Make It"	115
Where This Information Gets Us	117
Tools to Connect: Which of the four patterns do you have?	119

Section 5 The Darkness that Comes from Fear	**123**
All Negative Emotions Come from Fear	123
The Story- Darkness and Light	**125**
Living with Negative Emotions	126
How to Cope with Our Emotions	128
Releasing Your Emotions	130
Riding the Waves of Our Emotions to Release Them	131
Tools to Connect: Surfing Your Emotions	134
The Story- Quiet	**138**
Fear Is the Basis for All Destructive Actions and Behaviors	139
The Role of Distractions	140
Fear Is Only Overwhelming and Controlling When It is Repressed	143
The Story- A Daughter's Gifts	**144**
The Cascade of Darkness That Follows Fear	146
Tools to Connect: Connecting With Your Fears	151
Resistance to Letting Go of Our Fear and Darkness	159

Tools to Connect: Moving Through the Resistance	160
Learning to Let Go of Our Fears	166
Darkness is Contagious	168
Tools to Connect: Creating a Light Shield	171
Resistance to Changing the Dark Dance We Do with Others	178
Tools to Connect: Moving Through Resistance of Creating a Light Shield	181
Section 6: Making Sense of It and Moving Forward	**187**
When and How to Release Your Fear and Darkness	187
When and How to Connect with your Light	195
The Story- Hazel	**197**
Moving Forward and Choosing to Live Free of Fear	199
The Story- Butterflies	**201**

Preface

This book describes the journey that all humans take. It begins when we were small children filled with Light and meeting the world with Light. When we still believed that we were lovable and had value. We still saw and trusted in the goodness of others. We still felt the joy and excitement of simply being alive. It began to change as we learned to let fear and the negative emotions and behaviors, which are triggered by fear, define and control us.

Because this journey is one we all share, the pronoun *we* is used to express the idea that it is a journey that we all take. As you read the book, parts will resonate with you and make perfect sense and at those times the word *we* will feel like it includes *you*. However, there will also be sections that you will need to read a few times and reflect upon before you feel comfortable being a part of the collective *we*.

This book was written to create a path to help us reconnect with our Light, which we have hidden under our fear and the fears of others. Using the tools in this book, we will learn to recognize when we are afraid by noticing the negative emotions and hurtful behaviors that come from fear. We will learn to identify what we are afraid of and by doing so, reduce the power of our fear to negatively affect us. As we learn these skills, fear and the Darkness it creates will be no longer be in charge of how we think, feel, react, and behave. Instead, we will start loving and accepting ourselves as we begin focusing on the good in ourselves and in our friends, family, co-workers, and neighbors. By seeing the Light in others, they will, in turn, begin to see the good in themselves and so it will go.

In addition to explanations and tools, this book also contains short stories and art. The short stories are delineated with a different font and are on their own pages. We included both stories and art because they touch our hearts and minds differently than prose do.

The journey to living a happier life, filled with light, and guided by love is possible for anyone. All that is needed is an ability to reflect and learn and a motivation to change. As you read this book, allow yourself to move forward one small step at a time. Give yourself a chance to sit back and digest the words before you move on. You will need time and space to assimilate the ideas, the perspective, and the possibilities. Practice using the tools so they become an easy, natural, and automatic response to life's challenges.

Here's to all of us living in our Light, free at last from the tyranny of our fear and the fear of others!

Section 1

The Starting Place

Each of us entered the world open and trusting, small babies filled with Light. We were completely connected to that part of ourselves that feels joy, happiness, love, and the excitement of being alive at whatever level our individual minds were capable of experiencing. As we grew up, that light-filled part of ourselves, however, dimmed or seemed to get lost as we began to feel fear and to let that fear control us. We feared we would never be the person others needed, wanted, and expected us to be. We feared we would never be enough. We feared we would make mistakes and fail. As fear took over, our Light seemed to lose its importance and value. It's as if a light switch within us had been switched off. There we were in our Light, our happiness, and connection, and suddenly we found ourselves in the Dark, feeling negative emotions, behaving in hurtful ways, and focusing on what was wrong and bad in ourselves, others. We resigned ourselves to a life in the Dark, so much so that it is now familiar and normal. We have forgotten there ever was a Light switch as we learned to make do with living in the Dark. There are times when we have an unpredictable moment of Light, of happiness and joy that reminds us of our Light and of what we have seemingly lost. With no knowledge of our light switch, however, they remain rare and precious. This book is all about re-gaining control over that light switch so that we can flip from Darkness to Light once again and live in the Light if we so choose. It's that simple.

Who Are We?

Imagine looking in the mirror, who do you see looking back? It often isn't the person you long to see. It's not the you filled with sparkle and Light. The person looking back is the one you created from fear. The Light you long to see is still there, just hidden under your fear and the fears of others.

The Way We Change

When we are small children and first start experiencing fear, we look to our caregivers (the important people who care for us as children: parents, babysitters, family members, neighbors, teachers) to show us how to cope with it. We watch the way they respond when they are afraid and adopt many of their strategies. We are open to being directed by them to become the person they need and want us to be. These directives come in the form of a "How-To" book. Each of the important people in our lives has written their own book for us. These books lay out their rules, roles, and expectations for us. The clarity and the predictability of this information reduces our confusion as we try to please the important people in our lives and help them feel safe. We believe that as long as we follow the lessons laid out in the book that we will be loved and safe and will belong to our family and community.

Ropes

When a baby elephant is brought to the circus, trainers tame him by putting a rope around his neck and attaching the rope to a stake in the ground. The baby elephant is not strong enough to pull out the stake and so he learns to believe that the rope is stronger than he is. An elephant grows so quickly that in a short time, he could wrench that stake from the ground with the strength it takes a child to swat at a fly. But the elephant doesn't know this. He has been taught that the rope is stronger than he is, and he never thinks to question this fact. By the time he is an adult, he stands calmly with the rope around his neck attached to a stake (that he could demolish with a toenail), for years . . . for a lifetime.

Our Relationship with Fear

As humans, fear is biologically wired into us to help keep us safe and aid in our survival. We spend our lives on the lookout for fear and sometimes feeling it but mainly just reacting to it. The easiest way to know how much of our lives is spent in fear is by noticing how often we feel negative emotions. This is because all of our negative emotions are the result of fear. Close your eyes and think back on your day, your week, your life. How often have you been angry, sad, frustrated, lonely, resentful or any other negative emotion? It is so much more than it has to be. Is it more than you would desire it to be?

We accept this life of fear—feeling fear, responding to fear, and being controlled by it—because everyone we know lives this way. Our ability to know how to cope with fear has come from watching our caretakers and family respond to their fears and the fears of those around them. We have come to accept that fear is as inevitable as the hurt, anger, and other negative emotions that accompany it. We have resigned ourselves to believing that fear is our only option. It's sad we believe this and it is totally untrue. We do have other choices as we will learn. There are tools throughout the book to help us change so that living in our Light once again is not just a dream but a reality.

Eliora

Tools to Connect: A Meditation to Connect with Your Light

The first tool you will need is one which teaches you how to reconnect with your Light. Although it can feel like you may have lost your Light, it is still within you. It has just been hidden under all your changes in thinking, feeling, and perceiving that come from feeling fear. The first step to reconnecting with your Light is to keep your "thinking" mind busy. As you stop thinking, you have the space now to start being present in your body and can now begin to connect with who we are under all of the thinking, and the fear.

To make connecting with your Light even easier, you will focus on just one aspect of the breathing cycle: the exhalation. As you focus on your exhale, you are letting go. You are letting go of the air which has been depleted of oxygen. You are letting go of some of your stuck emotions and tension you are holding in your body. You are letting go of needing to be in control, and giving yourselves permission to relax.

As you continue to focus on your exhale, you will find that you are relaxing even more and that it feels like you dropping down and into your body. As you continue to let go, you will connect to the quiet core within you—your Light. This inner core is completely still and peaceful. The world, your emotions, and thoughts can be swirling around you and yet there is only peace and a feeling of safety as you connect to this part of yourself—your Light. In this space, you feel like you can finally feel the love, safety, and belonging that you have been searching for since you were born. You are home.

As you sit connected to this quiet core within you, you can watch your emotions and thoughts move across your conscious mind like clouds in the sky. As you watch their comings and goings, you can begin to recognize their transience. You can begin to understand that their presence doesn't define who you are. Instead, it is your Light, this inner core of peace that you can learn to count on as being your true you. Your Light is always constant and unchanging, like the sun. There are days and even weeks when the sun is covered with a thick layer of clouds. This does not mean the sun is not there, it is just hidden. As you meditate and focus on your exhale, you move through the clouds and no matter how thick the layer, you can reach the sun within you and feel its peace and love once again.

The Steps to Connecting with Your Light

1. Sit as tall as is comfortable, with your chest up and open. Partially or completely close your eyes. Rest your hands in your lap with your palms up and open. It can be helpful to rest them on a pillow if you find your chest falling forward as you meditate.

2. Notice the sounds and sensations of the air moving in and out of your body as you inhale and exhale. Notice the movement

of your chest, as it moves up and out as you inhale, and down and in as you exhale.

3. Now shift your focus to just your exhale—the sound of the air as it leaves your body, the feeling of the air as it moves out of your nose or mouth, the movement of your chest as it moves down and in. You can't help but notice when you are inhaling but all of your attention is on your exhale. Allow yourself to be filled up with and surrounded by the sensations of exhaling, so that there is no room for worry, thinking, remembering, planning.

4. As you focus on your exhale, what is shifting inside of you? Can you feel your body relaxing? Continue focusing on your exhale, allowing yourself to sink deeper and deeper into yourself. Can you feel the peace and the sense of safety as you connect with the quiet core within you?

5. As you focus on your exhale, there will be moments when you find yourself thinking. Please don't berate yourself. It is normal for your brain to think. When it happens, rest assured it will, just notice that your thoughts are wandering and gently bring your focus back to your exhale. It is important that you do this gently. There is no need to blame or shame yourself.

Your meditations will always be a mix of going back and forth between connecting with your breath and inner core and then thinking and then back again. The meditations in which you were able to connect more than think, you may label more successful. Those in which you spent the entire practice thinking, you may judge to be failures. It's understandable that you would think this way.

There is another way, however, to think about this struggle. Every moment you bring your focus back from thinking to connecting, you are learning that you can exert some level of control over your thoughts and emotions. As you watch them come and go across your conscious mind, you are learning to not define yourself by your thoughts and emotions. Lastly, you are learning that no matter how big or overwhelming your thoughts and emotions are, you can still choose to connect with your breath and Light. You are learning you always have a choice.

Be patient with yourself as you meditate. Over time, it will become easier to trust yourself and the process. There will be sessions or days when your meditation feels more of a struggle than a blessing. Those meditations when you spend more time thinking than connecting. We all do. Use those moments to practice choosing to reconnect with your breath and your Light.

It is with those moments of struggle that you can begin to understand the power of fear on your thoughts and emotions. Every time it feels impossible to sit and focus on your exhale because you feel agitated or overwhelmed, tell yourself that fear is the cause. When you simply make the connection in your mind that fear is triggering this reaction, it will subside and you will be able to slow down and meditate. By doing this, you can see firsthand the change that can come when you make the connection between feeling your negative emotions and recognizing that it is fear that is responsible for them.

Begin by trying to meditate for 5 minutes. A longer meditation does not necessarily equate with a better practice, or it being better for you, or being a better person, or even being better at helping you move forward and change. As you meditate, notice when you are thinking and gently bring your focus back to the sensations of exhaling. Remind yourself that each time you choose to let go of thinking and focus on your exhale, you are letting go of defining yourself by Darkness: your negative thoughts and emotions and especially your fears and the fears of the important people in your life. As you meditate, you are dropping below the fear and Darkness you both feel and manifest in your life. As you connect with the core of peace and Light within you, you are recognizing your fear and Darkness as separate from who you are deep inside.

Two Journeys

I heard a story once about a woman who was pronounced dead from a car accident. She remembered being lifted into an ambulance and hearing the paramedics who worked on her saying she was dead. "I'm here!" She tried to tell them. "I'm still here!" But they couldn't hear her. When they covered her with a sheet, she felt herself fly up off the stretcher and ascend into the air.

She could see miles of cars brought to a standstill on the highway, snaking all the way from the exit and on ramps. One car caught her attention—a brown sedan with a cracked back taillight. The car seemed to be pulsing with light. She went to this car. She could see perfectly.

She even noticed the license plate of this car. It was an Oklahoma plate. The woman in the car was praying. Praying for her! For the woman she'd seen flung from the car on the side of the road a little way back. The driver in the brown car squeezed her eyes shut and prayed, her lips moving quickly.

The flying woman hovered over the car and felt her body flood with light. In a flash, she was back in her body under the sheet. She was moving. Someone noticed her. "She's moving! She's alive!" The paramedics moved her to an ambulance where she was taken to the hospital and treated for her injuries.

While she recovered, she often thought about the woman in the brown car. When she was well enough to drive, she went to the DMV in Tulsa and inquired about the license plate. She was able to locate the address of the owner of the car. She bought a huge bouquet of flowers and drove to the woman's house. The brown car was in the driveway, the taillight was still cracked. She handed the woman the flowers and told her what she'd seen—the pulsing power of her prayers. She told the woman she was certain that the woman's prayers had saved her life. The woman's eyes grew big. She stepped backward into the house. It took her some time to speak. "We do things just because we're taught to do them. To be a good person. To try and help where we can. We don't believe they're real."

Eliora

Our Journey

We are each on our own journey that begins with our birth and ends in our death. Some aspects of our journey are unique to us, our memories, our families, our choices. Some aspects, however, are ones we all share. We all have the same basic emotional needs: to be safe, to feel loved, and to have a sense of belonging. We also all share the same ten foundational fears, including fearing we are not enough, we are failures if we make mistakes, or we will not belong. As we grow up, our shared goals are to get our needs met and to avoid feeling fear. It is the meeting of our needs and fears that causes us to change from living in the Light to living in the Dark.

Our first step on this journey was being born into a family. Our family is a group of people who may be related to us or not, and who by choice care for us. We all entered the world connected to our joy, our Light, our love for ourselves and others. We were born believing: anything is possible; we are extraordinary; we are lovable and likeable; and that life and the world are welcoming us with open arms. We experienced this at whatever level our individual minds were capable. This way of being and feeling may have lasted days, months, or years depending on our family and life circumstance as well as the traumas we experienced

As we continue to mature, we begin to understand that our caregivers and families have expectations that we must meet to ensure their continued love, acceptance, and caring. The older and more independent we become, the more we begin to recognize and respond to the expectations of our neighborhoods, schools, religious organizations, and communities. Each person and each group have their own expectations of us that they require us to meet, as defined by their How-To books. These expectations vary and depend in part on their culture, gender, race, and socioeconomic level. These books teach us how to be like them, to fit in with them, to play by and live by their rules, and to play the roles they have assigned us. Unfortunately, each time we change who we are to meet another person's expectation of us, we limit and restrict ourselves. With each change, we become less connected to our Light and more convinced that we aren't enough or that we are lacking. By focusing on our fears and responding to other people's fears, we lose sight of our Light. The truth is that it is always still within us burning bright, hidden under fear and Darkness.

As we try to understand our journey through life it's important to remind ourselves that our caretakers are human. They, like all of us, are a mix of Light and Dark. There were times when our caretakers were in their Light and saw and focused on the good in us and felt love and compassion for us. There were also times, however, when they were caught up in their own fears and overwhelmed with negative emotions which caused them to say unkind words to us, to reject us, and to possibly hurt us. Their fears also pushed them to create expectations that they demanded we meet. The sole purpose of their expectations is to help protect them from feeling fear. Understanding the effects of our caretaker's Darkness on our own fears can help us understand some of the reasons we developed into who we are now. As we understand the effects of their fears on who we have become, it is important to not focus on blaming or finding fault with them. It's about acknowledging how we reacted to their fears, so that we can make choices about who we want to be now.

Lessons in Belonging

When Patricia was young, she pushed away the pancakes, the meatloaf, the brisket with its rivulets of flesh.

"I like zucchini, eggplant, and jaunty peas rolled in butter," she said.

"Kids are starving in Rwanda," her parent said and told her to clean her plate.

One night, after being forced to eat a piece of steak (an event which took three hours) her parent said, "I hope you learned your lesson."

Patricia had learned her lesson. She learned not to listen to her body. She ate whatever was offered to her. The steak sandwich and tater tots and French bread pizza at school. At home, the ham, the beef stew, the bone-in chicken. After school before her parents came home, she ate mini-coffee cakes, crinkly bags of cookies, ice cream, pretzels, ruffled chips (sweet with sour cream and onion flavoring), translucent bags of Swedish fish, and licorice whips from the store that sold things in bulk family sizes. She learned to fill her body with crunch, with the silt of sugar granules, until there was nothing but sweet emptiness, and she didn't have to feel anything at all.

Section 2

Learning to Live with Fear

Do you ever wonder who you would be had if you had grown up under different circumstances perhaps in a different family or culture or society? At some level, we all understand the influence our family and society has had on who we have become. Their influence is, in part, determined by how filled with fear or connected to their Light they were. For they, like us, are a mix of Dark and Light, of fear and love. A state of being that changes minute to minute depending on what is happening to us, around us, and within us. It changes depending on how much fear we are feeling and how much fear others around us are feeling at that moment in our life. Our fear and the fears of others are the controlling factor that determines whether we grew up surrounded by and living in our Light or the Dark.

Eliora

Making Changes

Being in our Light means we feel compassion not only for ourselves but for others as well. When our caregivers are in their Light, it greatly influences how they interact with us. When they feel safe being themselves, they can let go of their expectations of us and want only the best for us. When they are in their Light, they don't need anything from us and so can love and accept who we are and who we are not. We then feel safe, knowing deep down inside that they see our value. We can trust that the other person's intentions come from their desire to help us from love rather than to control us with fear. We leave these interactions brighter and lighter. We feel loved and accepted for who we are. We feel connected to our Light and inspired to be the most loving and compassionate person we can possibly be to ourselves and to others.

Just as our caretakers are loving and supportive when they are in Light, so they can also be critical and rejecting when they are filled with fear. As their fear causes them to feel unsafe, their expectations of us, created to protect them from fear, increase in both number and intensity. When we don't meet their expectations, they not only feel the fear they were trying to avoid, but also feel a sense of betrayal that we didn't care enough to put their need to feel safe first.

When we were young and first exposed to expectations, we responded in two ways; we met them or we couldn't meet them.

When we met the expectations of our caretakers and received their positive responses, we learned this was an easy way of helping our caregivers feel calm and safe and to feel good about ourselves as well. When we didn't meet their expectations, it was usually because we were incapable. At this young age, we wanted to please our caregivers and when we didn't, we immediately feared it is because we were bad, wrong, unlovable, unlikable, worthless, not enough.

Either response resulted in us restricting who we believed we needed to be so we could either please others or avoid feeling the fear that there was something wrong with us. When we were able to meet their expectations, we were adhering to the rules, roles, and expectations they laid out for us in the How-To book. Their responses to us let us know that we succeeded in helping them feel safe, loved, and a sense of belonging. They showed this by telling us that they were pleased with us and saw us as lovable and acceptable. Each of these moments when we met an expectation becomes a "snapshot", which we could study repeatedly, gleaning as much information as we could about how we needed to be to be acceptable to this person.

Just as we have snapshots when we met expectations, we also have other snapshots of when we didn't. These were the moments when we upset, angered, or frustrated our caregivers by not meeting their expectations. We didn't follow the rules, the roles, or the expectations of who they needed us to be to feel safe. Each of us has a pile of these snapshots of unmet expectations, which we studied even more carefully as we tried to understand what we did wrong and how we could change to be seen as good and accepted.

Our goals as young children were to be accepted and if possible loved by our caretakers so that they continue to care for us and protect us. The key to this process was learning how to make our caregivers feel safe being with us. They felt safe when they felt competent, relaxed, in control, and able to anticipate how we would respond. Often, they would feel safest when we seemed to be just like them. By reducing their fear, we also hoped this would help us avoid situations that triggered fear in us. These changes and restrictions we imposed on ourselves were the first steps to creating our own Suit of Darkness to help protect us from fear.

Creating Expectation for Others

We spend our lives trying to feel safe, which can only happen when we avoid feeling fear. One important way we do this is to ask the important people in our lives to help protect us from our fears. Just as others have expectations of us to feel safe, we also create expectations for others so that we will feel less fear. For example, in our important (core) relationships we may expect others to reassure us that we are important, that we matter, that they won't leave us, and that we belong with them. They may express this by choosing us over others, remembering our birthdays, or verbally affirming how much they love us. When they meet our expectations, we feel safe, important, loved, and that we belong for at least that moment. Unfortunately, by creating expectations for others, we have handed over our safety to them. As a result, we are constantly worried that those we rely on to protect us from fear will choose not to meet our expectations.

Whenever other people don't meet our expectations, there is a sense that they have failed us and betrayed our trust. For rather than protecting us, they have forced us to feel the very fears we were trying to avoid. Think about the people in your closest relationships and the expectations you have for them. Do you need them to make you a priority, to remember you on your Birthday, submit to your control? Extend the circle and think about the people you work with or live next to, what expectations do you have for them? Each of these expectations was created from fear in our hopes to avoid fear. What are the fears you are trying to avoid by creating these expectations?

Take a moment and remember when one of your expectations was not met. How did you respond? What fear did it trigger in you? Were there harsh words or perhaps guilting or blaming? All those negative words and reactions show us clearly that fear is the basis of our expectations. As we begin to make the connection in our minds between the presence of fear and the creation of our expectations and our reliance on them, a shift begins to happen within us. They begin to loosen their hold over us and we can begin to rely on them a bit less and to feel less threatened when they are not met.

Dreams

Sometimes our soul awakens to a vision—to something bigger that we're here to be, to do, to create. These visions are who we really are, but we can't see this because we're under a spell. We tell ourselves we're not capable, not worthy, not something enough, or too something or other. We tell ourselves it's enough to enjoy the vision—to dream about doing those things.

"This way," we say, "no one gets hurt. No feathers get ruffled."

Sometimes, we might even start to talk about the dream. It's fun to do this with certain friends. We say "one day" we'll go for it, but we remain too afraid. We're so afraid we won't even admit to ourselves that we're afraid.

We don't say "I'm scared out of my skin!" but I'm going to make that call, take that chance, talk to that person, put myself up for that job, start that relationship, go on that trip.

My friend said this is like eating the physical menu instead of the food. We become "menu eaters" and forget that cardboard and plastic are nothing like herbs, sauteed butter, ribbons of pasta, and fish right out of the ocean.

Fear Versus Love

Some people equate having expectations for someone as being the same as wanting the best for them. They see their expectations as important gifts they give their children and loved ones. For without expectations, they fear their children won't know how to fit in or succeed.

Having expectations for someone, however, is very different from wanting the best for them. We can tell the difference between the two by our responses. If we are wanting only the best for someone, we may feel happy or sad for the person when it happens or doesn't happen, but their successes or failures does not reflect on us. We don't feel safer or more fearful because of their experiences.

Expectations are just the opposite. When an expectation is not met, it causes a strong emotional response in us. We feel not only disappointed, hurt, betrayed but we feel the very fear we were hoping to avoid. Simply put, you know it's an expectation if you feel punished when the person it was designed for doesn't meet it. Fear is the reason we create expectations, why we believe we need them, and why we respond so negatively when they are not met.

The Effects of Fear

Babies enter the world small beings filled with Light. They first begin to experience fear when they feel lonely, hurt, pain, uncomfortable, perhaps rejected. Fear is an extremely powerful emotion because it triggers both an emotional and physiological response in our bodies. Like all vertebrates, when we feel fear, there is an immediate fight or flight response in our body believing our survival is threatened. In those moments, fear is fulfilling its evolutionary purpose by helping us to fight or run away from a threat. It's helping us stay alive and to reproduce and pass on our genes to the next generation.

For many of us, the majority of our fear doesn't come from being in danger. It comes instead from the ordinary upsets of living, such as being late for a meeting at work, your child having a tantrum in public, or getting a stain on your favorite shirt. Even though these moments are annoying, embarrassing, or upsetting, we still respond to the situation as if our survival was threatened. Our fear response takes its cue from the adrenaline coursing through our body. Our mind begins to think perhaps there is something wrong and we actually do need to be afraid. Our imagination begins to embellish how much fear we are feeling, making it even bigger and more powerful than it is. As our fears become larger and scarier, they begin to negatively impact our thinking, perspective, emotions, and behaviors. When we can objectively see our fears for what they truly are, not what we imagine they are, they lose their ability to overwhelm and control us.

Our Shared Fears

All humans share ten Foundational Fears. These are the fears that get triggered whenever anything upsetting happens in our life. They are the ones that motivate us to change and restrict who, what, and how we are in response to our caregivers, social institutions, and traumas. They are the ones that trigger Darkness within us: our negative emotions, hurtful behaviors, and our focus on what is bad and wrong. They are the fears that control us and cause us to hide our Light.

The Ten Foundational Fears

1. **Failing**. The fear that we will fail, make mistakes, or get something wrong. The fear we will be judged, rejected, and condemned by ourselves and by others for failing, making mistakes, or getting something wrong.

2. **Abandonment**. The fear that those we care for and who care for us will stop loving us. They may abandon us, leave us, die, or choose to walk away.

3. **Being Deprived**. The fear that we won't get what we think we want and need from others, from life, from the world, or from the Divine.

4. **Not Belonging**. The fear that we won't belong, we don't belong, we will never belong, or that we won't be invited to

belong. Belonging means feeling loved, accepted, and safe with another person or a group of people.

5. **Not Enough**. The fear that who we are is not enough: not good enough, smart enough, attractive enough, important enough, or happy enough, etc. The fear that we are not enough of the person that others, life, the world need, want, require, and/or expect us to be.

6. **Worthless**. The fear that who we are deep down inside is a monster, that we are nothing or a nobody or that we are broken and defective. We fear that we are worthless, useless, unlovable, unlikable, and undesirable.

7. **Meaningless**. The fear that who we are and what our lives are is meaningless and purposeless.

8. **Unimportant**. The fear that we aren't important or don't matter to other people, to life, to the world, or to the Divine.

9. **External Changes**. The fear of losing what we already have—such as our possessions, relationships, people, pets, status, etc.

10. **Internal Changes**. The fear that how we see, know, or define ourselves will change and be lost. Our roles and labels will disappear. This also includes how we need and want other people in the world to see, know, and define us.

These ten fears are present in every person. We feel them when we become convinced that they are actually true, that we are broken, or unimportant or not enough. For example, perhaps we believe we have been treated unfairly and we fear it is because we are not enough (Foundational Fear #5). As that fear fills us, we start to focus on what is wrong with us, all the ways we aren't not enough, and all the moments in our lives when we have let others down by not being enough. Each time we find another reason to see ourselves as not enough, the fear becomes even more powerful within us.

Tools to Connect: **Connecting with the Light in Children**

It's especially important that we remind ourselves of our Light and connect with it when we are afraid and filled with Darkness. The greatest source of Light in the world is in small children because they haven't begun the process of hiding their Light under fear. As you watch small children play, create, and enjoy life, you are connecting to their Light. Just thinking about the joy or love so easily expressed by a small child can remind you of and help you reconnect with your own Light.

Steps to Connecting to the Light in Children

1. Sit as tall as is comfortable, with your chest up and open. Partially or completely close your eyes. Rest your hands in your lap with your palms up and open. It can be helpful to rest them on a pillow if you find your chest falling forward as you meditate.
2. Notice the sounds and sensations of the air moving in and out of your body as you inhale and exhale. Notice the movement of your chest, as it moves up and out as you inhale, and down and in as you exhale.
3. Now shift your focus to just your exhale—the sound of the air as it leaves your body, the feeling of the air as it moves out of your nose or mouth, the movement of your chest as it moves down and in. You can't help but notice when you are inhaling

but all of your attention is on your exhale. Allow yourself to be filled up with and surrounded by the sensations of exhaling, so that there is no room for worry, thinking, remembering, planning.

4. Think of a child filled with happiness and joy, who is simply excited to be alive. It could be you when you were young or any a child you have known or seen. The joy, happiness, and excitement they radiate is their Light. Think of a child swinging on a swing or dancing freely and with abandon. Think of a child seeing the beauty of a flower or successfully building a tower of blocks. These are often moments when you can see and feel their Light.

5. As you think of this child, notice how you are feeling inside. Can you feel the shift as it connects to your Light? You may find yourself smiling, laughing, or feeling more relaxed and able to refocus on the positives in yourself and in your life. You may feel less overwhelmed with fear and able to just enjoy the memory, the moment. Create a collection of these memories you can go back to whenever you want to connect with your Light.

6. Take a minute and look through old photos from your life or look online at photos of children. Look for images that make you smile and feel happy, or loved or uplifted. Keep them in a place you can look at them again and again. By connecting to that moment captured in the photo, you can connect with your Light no matter how afraid or Dark you are feeling.

Fear and Our Suit of Darkness

Whenever any of the 10 Foundational Fears are triggered in us, we lose a little bit more trust and belief in the validity of our Light, in our goodness, lovability, and worth. For example, when we are excluded from fun, we may suddenly fear it may be because there is something wrong with us, perhaps we are defective in some way. We may fear that we made a mistake and now we are being rejecting for it. We may fear that our dearest friend no longer loves us and no longer wants to spend time with us. As we begin to believe that any one of these fears is the reason we were excluded, we become more and more focused on our fear. We begin to believe that it is our Darkness rather than our Light that defines who we really are. As a result, our Light dims in importance to us as we begin to live in Darkness: feeling negative emotions, behaving in hurtful ways, and focusing only on the negative.

All the ways we respond to fear become our Suit of Darkness. Each piece of this suit has been carefully constructed in response to a fear, or to an expectation placed on us by others. It contains all the restrictions we have adopted as we tried to become the person our families and communities wanted, needed, and expected us to be. Its sole purpose is help us avoid feeling even more fear. We put on our suit every moment we have felt fear. As a result, our suit feels safe and familiar; it has become part of who we are and how we see ourselves. When we look in the mirror often who we see is this suit of Darkness created from fear.

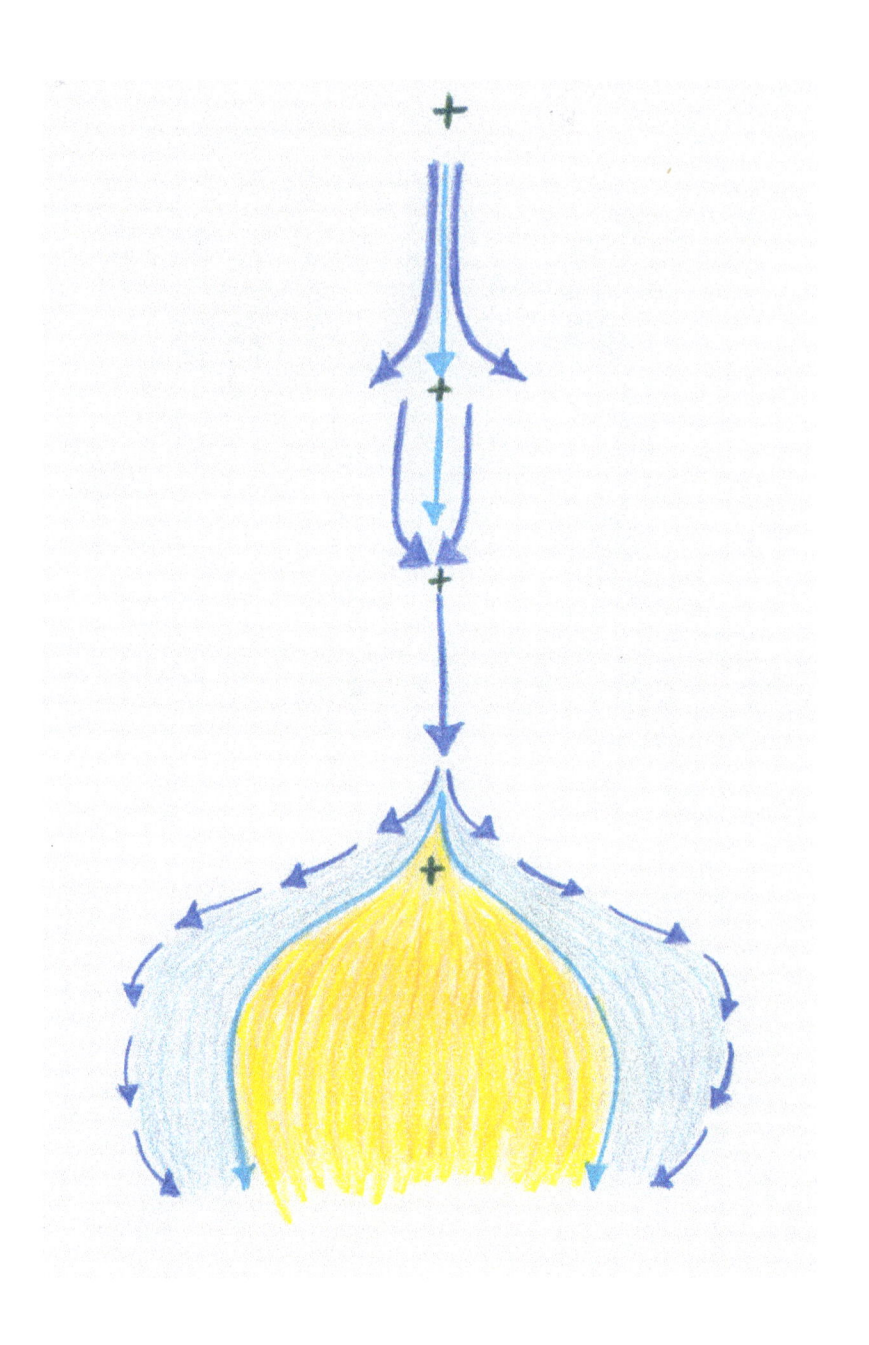

Our Dance with Fear

Our dance with fear began when we were small, for some as of us as small as newborn infants. We were born open to seeing and knowing the world from a place of innocence, joy, and Light. We had little if any experience with fear. We were dependent on others to care for us. We thrived when we were loved, shown affection, and held. Yet, there were also moments when we felt pain and the discomfort of hunger, thirst, or loneliness. This triggered fear in us which we hadn't learned to cope with yet. We didn't know how to make it stop or how to avoid it. Our relationship with fear was to try to simply make it go away. We did this by expressing our upset as fussiness, neediness, irritability, and agitation until our needs were met. Once we are fed, held, comforted, cared for, or loved, the fear subsided, and we once again felt safe.

Growing up in an unpredictable and uncontrollable world, we relied on our caregivers and families to help us be and feel safe. We knew immediately when they felt happy and in their Light and when they were afraid. It was in those moments when they were in their Light that we felt cherished, loved, and supported. We knew when they felt fear because they became impatient and angry with us and maybe even rejected us. They became more demanding in their expectations of us. They expressed their fear as Dark emotions, behaviors, and expectations which triggered fear in us as well.

We grew up believing that to be safe and protected from other people's Darkness, their negative emotions, and hurtful behaviors, we must let their fears define us. We did this by changing our sense of self with respect to their expectations. We tried to become quieter or more boisterous, more academic or less academic, less successful or more successful, whatever they needed us to be so that they felt safe. Their fear became our fear and controlled who we could be in relationship with ourselves and others, with life and the world. In doing so, we seemingly lost connection to the parts of ourselves that lit us up, allowed us to create with joy and passion, and to love and trust ourselves.

Every change we have made to avoid triggering fear in others and in ourselves has resulted in the creation of our custom-made Suit of Darkness. This suit has been fabricated with all the fears we have taken in and on from others. Its cut and tightness come from the restrictions we have imposed on ourselves in response to fear. It's heaviness and weight come from the expectations we have created for others in the hopes they will now protect us from fear. With this suit, we hope to have the ability to avoid fear, both our own and other people's.

By learning about fear and its role in our lives, we have reached a new crossroads on our journey. We can continue letting fear control our lives, pushing us to create expectations, expressing Dark emotions and behaviors as well as continuing to restrict who we are allowed to be in the world. Or we can choose to recognize and release our fears and by doing so reconnect with our Light, seeing the good in ourselves and others. We can learn to have compassion for other people's fears and no longer respond to their fear by becoming afraid ourselves. When we are connected to our Light, we can immediately feel any fear we are holding onto so that we can choose to let it go. We can see its negative effects on our thoughts, emotions, behavior, and interactions. We can see our fears for what they truly are, just reactions to the upsets of life; not the life threatening and dangerous emotions our imaginations have blown them up to be. In this way, we can now learn to look at our fears objectively so that they diminish in power and lose their ability to fill our lives with Darkness.

When we are in our Light, it is like we have switched our old pair of glasses, the ones with dark scratched lenses, for a new pair of glasses with clear lenses. What we once saw as dark, monochromatic, and distortive, we can now see is multicolored, bright, light, and clear. With these new glasses, everyone and everything we look at looks lighter and brighter. Our ability to see and thus our perspective changes as a result of these new glasses. We no longer need to see everything as just Dark, for now we can see the Light as well.

Tools to Connect: **Listening to the Quiet Voice Within**

There is within you a quiet voice that comes from your Light. This voice is from the part of you that loves and accepts yourself and sees your value. Most of our life, we only hear the voice of our "thinking" mind, which is heavily influenced by fear. This is the voice that tells you don't bother trying because you will only get hurt or that you aren't enough or that you will just fail. As the voice of your fearful self becomes louder and more important to you, it eventually overwhelms and drowns out the soft voice of your Light. To once again hear the voice of your Light, the voice of your "thinking" mind needs to be quieted. With time and practice, the voice of your Light—also called your Deepest Wisdom—will become louder, clearer, and more of a presence in your life.

The first step to learning to listen to your Light is to slow down and focus on your exhale so that you can begin letting go of the worries and cares of life. When you focus on your exhale (the sounds and sensations of breathing out), you begin to relax. You begin to once again trust that you have value, that you are lovable and enough. This process of letting go helps us again begin to feel safe, loved, and held which reconnects us our Light—the most loving and giving part of who we are.

Focusing on our exhale is also very effective at quieting the "noise" of our thinking to better hear our Deepest Wisdom.

It keeps our "thinking" mind so busy, it doesn't have time to answer the questions we are asking our Deepest wisdom. This is why it is so important to focus your "thinking" mind on your exhale the entire time you are connecting to and receiving from Deepest Wisdom.

The voice of our Deepest Wisdom can come in many forms: images, words, music, emotions, or a memory. As we practice asking our Deepest Wisdom questions and then "listening" for the response, the answers come more readily, clearer to hear, and easier to understand. It's like listening to a radio. As we learn where and how to tune in the radio, the signal becomes clearer and after a while, we are able to tune into the station easily and automatically.

Being Guided by the Quiet Voice Within

1. Spend a few moments thinking of a question you would like to ask your Deepest Wisdom. Try to make it clear and concise. Questions that are fuzzy and unclear create responses that are fuzzy and unclear. It can be helpful to write the question down so you can refer back to it when you are ready to ask it.
2. Sit as tall as is comfortable, with your chest up and open. Partially or completely close your eyes. Rest your hands in your lap with your palms up and open. It can be helpful to rest them on a pillow if you find your chest falling forward as you meditate.

3. Notice the sounds and sensations of the air moving in and out of your body as you inhale and exhale. Notice the movement of your chest, as it moves up and out as you inhale, and down and in as you exhale.

4. Now shift your focus to just your exhale—the sound of the air as it leaves your body, the feeling of the air as it moves out of your nose or mouth, the movement of your chest as it moves down and in. You can't help but notice when you are inhaling but all of your attention is on your exhale. Allow yourself to be filled up with and surrounded by the sensations of exhaling, so that there is no room for worry, thinking, remembering, planning.

5. Notice you are relaxing into your body. Your mind is becoming quieter and more peaceful as you focus on your exhale. Allow the sensations of breathing out to consume your attention so that there is no room left for thinking or worrying. Let the sensations fill you up and surround you.

6. Once you feel relaxed and at peace within your body, read or think of the question you want to ask your Deepest Wisdom.

7. As soon as you ask your question, go back to focusing on your exhale. To hear the quiet whisper that comes from your Deepest Wisdom, you must make space for it to be heard. It's absolutely necessary therefore to keep your thinking mind occupied so that it does not overwhelm the softer voice of Deepest Wisdom. Continue focusing on your exhale as you wait to receive the "pop" from Deepest Wisdom. A pop is different

from a thinking answer because it doesn't come from reflection, remembering, or cogitating it, it just appears, all on its own. Often when you receive a pop, it is accompanied by a sigh, and feeling of relief. It's as if your body suddenly relaxes because you now have the answer that Deepest Wisdom has been trying to tell you.

8. The answer can be in the form of words, ideas, images, memories, feelings, or even songs. Write down whatever answer you receive. It may not make sense yet but that is OK because with a few more questions and answers, the message will become clearer.

9. Some examples of follow-up questions include: What does this answer mean to me? Is there another way to look at this answer that will help me understand it? What am I missing in my understanding of this answer? Each time you get an answer, write it down.

10. Learning to listen and receive input from your Deepest Wisdom takes time and practice. It is well worth the effort because you will have an internal source of guidance that comes from a part of you that believes in you, loves and accepts you, and will not let fear shut you down.

Section 3

Protecting Ourselves from Fear:

Ours and Other People's

Understanding Our Suit of Darkness

Anytime we anticipate fear, ours or someone else's, we immediately put on our Suit of Darkness to help us avoid feeling more of it. The sole purpose of this suit is protection, not comfort. As a result, sometimes the suit can feel heavy and cumbersome. It tends to restrict our movements, and our ability to connect. These liabilities, however feel unimportant when we sense fear is lurking nearby in us or someone else, waiting to overwhelm and control us.

There are three main sources of fear in our lives. The first is other people's fear. When they feel fear, they express it by getting angry, feeling anxious, rejecting, shutting down, or a host of other Dark emotions and behaviors. They also express their fear as expectations so that their fears become our problem, our responsibility and we are expected to do whatever they need to keep them safe. When others are filled with fear, their fear has the potential to trigger any or all of the ten Foundational Fears in us.

To understand how the fears of others trigger fears in us, imagine a small child who believes they have created a masterpiece of art with markers and paint on the fresh clean walls of their bedroom. They are filled with the joy and excitement of creation, and of playing with colors and textures and design. Imagine their caregiver walking into their room and seeing this "mess". Imagine the expectations of the caregiver that haven't been met. Imagine the fears that are triggered in the caregiver as a result of the child choosing to create on a wall rather than on paper. Imagine the negative emotions and hurtful behaviors that are expressed towards the young child and how the child feels as a result. Lastly imagine the fear(s) that now fill this small child.

The second source of fear is our internal fear. It is the fear we carry within us and constantly worry that it is true. Foundational Fear #6 (the fear I am Worthless) is always on our minds. We go through life hunting vigilantly for any reason that it might be true, that we are or might be worthless, broken, defective, unlovable, unlikeable, or, even worse, a monster, or that others will see and judge us this way. Once we have found proof that we are any of those terrible things is true or might be true, we are filled with this fear.

We first experienced this fear when we were very young and started to compare ourselves to others. Imagine a 2-year-old, who believes they can run as fast as the wind, racing an older sibling and being left far behind. What do they believe about themselves now?

These fears are also brought into being when we don't live up to other people's expectations and they hurt us in response. Imagine a hungry, overtired 3-year-old losing it and having a tantrum in the grocery store. In response, their poor parent, who is mortified and afraid of what others will say and think saying to them, "I don't love you when you behave like this".

The message to the child in both cases is there is something wrong with you. In the first instance the child now believes they aren't the person they thought they were, instead they can see that they lacking. In the second instance, the child now believes they are no longer lovable, and likeable, perhaps even that they are a monster. Foundational Fear #6 is a major source of internal fear and is lurking within us every moment of every day looking for reasons to be triggered.

The third source of fear comes from living in a world which is ever changing and so feels unpredictable and out of our control. These are the changes of growing up, growing old, and dying. The changes that come from losing jobs, friends, and health. The fear and overwhelm that come with the change of loved ones moving away, leaving the relationship, or dying. So many changes and each one triggering fear in us. It could be any or all of the 10 Foundational Fears that are triggered as a result of the changes we experience in ourselves, other people, relationships, life, and the world. To help us cope with the fear that comes from constant change, we look to our caregivers for guidance as to the best way to respond. We learn their ways and make them our own.

Each time we feel fear and reject a part of who we are, restrict who we are allowed to be, or adopt someone else's coping technique, we add to our Suit of Darkness. The sole purpose of this suit is to help us live our lives unscathed by more fear. We think our suit is actually who we are, but it's just something we have learned to put on to be safe. It hides our true self, the self we entered the world as and were born to be. It hides our Light.

These Lessons are Stored Deep in Our Subconscious

For a small child, life is filled with precious moments of joy, love, and connections with their bodies, with nature, and with the world. Life could also feel scary and overwhelming when it changed, when we didn't get what we needed, and when the people around us got angry and then punished, rejected, and hurt us. As young children we had no idea of how to respond or stay safe in situations like this. We looked to our caregivers to teach us their ways of coping and of behaving. Our caregivers were our everything, the center of our worlds. We studied their every move, their moods, their words, their reactions to fear in themselves, fear in others, and fear from life and the world. We believed if their reactions kept them safe, they would keep us safe as well.

The lessons we learned, watching and adopting our caregiver's reactions to fear, are safely stored inside of us. The restrictions we took on as a result of their expectations and from our own fears are stored within us as well. We create and accumulate these lessons, one at a time from our families, society, and life experiences, in the form of subconscious beliefs. Each time we create or learn a new belief, we limit and shut down another part of ourselves until sometimes it can be hard to remember the person who originally entered the world.

As we grow up, these subconscious beliefs influence who, what, and how we exist in the world. They control how we respond, how we see ourselves, and how others see us. Our subconscious beliefs are different from our conscious ones. We are aware of the beliefs stored in our conscious mind. When someone asks us what we believe, our answers come from our conscious beliefs. Subconscious beliefs are stored in a part of our brain we can't access, and so we are not aware of them. We know of their existence only by observing their effects on our thinking and our behaviors. Unlike the conscious beliefs that change as we grow and evolve, our subconscious beliefs stay the same throughout our lifetime. The subconscious beliefs we created at four are still with us at eighty.

There are three types of protective subconscious beliefs: Legacy Beliefs learned from our caregivers, Societal Beliefs based on the rules of society, and Trauma-Induced Beliefs created in response to traumatic life experiences. The sole purpose of each of these types of belief is to protect us by restricting and limiting who we are allowed to be in the world so that we can avoid feeling fear.

Legacy Beliefs

Legacy Beliefs were created to ensure our survival. These beliefs are especially important to us as they have a proven track record of helping our caretakers avoid fear and survive to become adults. As a result, we believe they are essential for our survival as well. We "inherit" these beliefs from our primary caretakers at a subconscious level, so we aren't even aware we have adopted them.

Each Legacy Belief was created in response to a specific type of situation and to the specific fears that are triggered in it. These beliefs have been handed down the generations to help us know how to cope with that situation and its fears. When we find ourselves in these situations and feeling these fears, the legacy beliefs created to respond to them are activated and begin to control how we think, feel, and behave.

Unlike the color of your hair, which is determined by the inheritance of genes, these subconscious beliefs are not passed on biologically. Rather, they are subconsciously adopted as we observe how our caregiver feels, thinks, and behaves in response to fear. In general, we do not take on all of our caregiver's Legacy Beliefs, but rather we adopt some from one caregiver and others from a second or even a third. We are open to accepting these beliefs from any person who has played a vital role in our lives as small children.

Hand-Me-Down

*I*heard a story about a woman who was very poor as a child. When she was thirteen, she was given a hand-me-down dress from Goodwill. The dress was small, so she had to hold her arms close to her body and hunch up at her neck to get the sleeves on. The dress had one sleeve shorter than the other. The fabric was coarse and thick and made a swish, swish sound everywhere she went, announcing her presence like a squeaky wheel.

Eventually the woman made her way out into the world. She found a job she liked and saved enough money to buy a new dress. She had the dress custom made, the floral fabric burst with color and fit her body perfectly, not too long, the sleeves just right. But she couldn't stand to wear it. Her arms felt awkward and dangly at her sides. The silent soft fabric felt wispy and paper thin and offered her no protection at all. She sensed people staring at her oddly on the street, glancing once and twice out of the side of their eyes. Within a week she was holding her arms close and hunched up at the odd angle, until the new dress conformed to the familiar shape.

Legacy Beliefs continued

All Legacy Beliefs share the same beginning: *To be safe, I must always, or I must never . . .*

The purpose of these beliefs is to restrict how we see ourselves and who we can be in the world in order to avoid fear. Some examples are:

- To be safe, when I am afraid that I won't get what I want and need, I must always be in control.
- To be safe, when I am afraid that I have made a mistake or gotten something wrong, I must always blame myself.
- To be safe, when I am afraid that I am worthless or unlovable, I must always be the person others want, need, and expect me to be.
- To be safe, when I am afraid that I don't or won't belong to a group, I must never acknowledge or express any of my negative emotions.

Legacy Beliefs vary from person to person and are the basis for our individual differences and how we present ourselves to the world. They are key components of our Suit of Darkness. Our Legacy Beliefs are activated and start to limit and restrict us whenever we feel the fear that inspired their creation. Because they are stored in our subconscious, we aren't aware of them and only know they are there by the effects they have on our thoughts, emotions, responses, behaviors, and life choices.

Our Societal Beliefs

Every community or society has rules concerning the behavior they expect their members to follow. Many of these rules are absolutely necessary for the safety of the society, such as the rules governing destructive and anti-social behaviors like murder, robbery, etc. Other rules are more arbitrary and have been created to keep power in the hands of a specific subset of the population. They determine which groups are at the top of the social and power hierarchy and which ones are at the bottom. They determine the roles which different sexes, genders, races, ages, cultures, and castes are allowed to play.

As children, we were subjected to society's rules and regulations both in our families and in societal institutions. These institutions included our schools, places of worship, and cultural centers. It also included the television and movies we watched, the social media and internet we engaged with, and the books and newspapers we read. From each of these places, we learned who we needed to be, to be accepted by our families, the local community, and broader society.

As young children, we learned to take in and absorb these rules at both a conscious and subconscious level in order to fit in and be safe. Our conscious beliefs have changed and grown as we have changed and grown. Our subconscious beliefs, however, have remained exactly the same as when we first adopted them. They are a constant. These subconscious beliefs have defined who we believe we are allowed to be in our families and society. These beliefs are strongly influenced by the rules of the culture. Some examples are:

- A good woman is one who cares for others by putting others' needs first.
- People of color don't deserve the same benefits as people who are white.
- A person with money is superior to someone who lacks it.

Our Trauma-Induced Beliefs

When we experience a trauma, our priority is to ensure we will never feel that level of pain and suffering again. In these moments when we are overwhelmed with fear and negative emotions, we create a subconscious belief to protect ourselves by placing draconian restrictions and limitations on who, what, and how we can be. We believe that if we reject the part of ourselves that was harmed by the trauma, then we will be protected if the trauma should be repeated. Our hope is that by doing so, we can avoid experiencing such overwhelming fear and its resulting devastation.

These beliefs take the form of *I am or I don't* followed by the protective restriction. Some common examples are:

- I am stupid.
- I don't deserve to be loved.
- I am ugly.
- I am worthless.

We create these beliefs in the hope that if we are already telling ourselves we are stupid, ugly, or unlovable, we will be less devastated if that part of ourselves is ever attacked again.

What determines if an experience is traumatic is not how it necessarily appears to others, but how destructive it feels to us. Violence, death, verbal abuse, abandonment all create traumas but so do smaller seemingly inconsequential events like forgetting your homework or being left out of a party. Whether it is traumatic or not depends on how the person who is coping with the fears perceives it. If it is overwhelming and results in the creation of a Trauma-induced belief, then it is considered a trauma in this book.

The role of these Trauma-Induced Beliefs, much like the Legacy and Societal Beliefs, is to keep us safe, by limiting how we see ourselves and how others see us as well. We do it, however, by creating subconscious beliefs that decimate an aspect of ourselves to ensure we will never be crushed by such a blow to that particular aspect of ourselves again.

Tools to Connect: Reliving Past Moments of Light

When we are in our Darkness, feeling sad, angry, frustrated, alone, we struggle to remember that we even have a Light. We might be aware that there have been moments of happiness and love in our lives, but we truly can't remember them. They are like faded photos from our past that have no real substance, just a label written in pencil on the back—Happy Day Spent at the Beach. This tool is to help you recover your connection to those moments. As you relive those memories, all the happiness and Light can come flooding back to you. You will once again be reminded of the Light you have within you hidden under your Suit of Darkness.

Meditation for Remembering

1. Sit as tall as is comfortable, with your chest up and open. Partially or completely close your eyes. Rest your hands in your lap with your palms up and open. It can be helpful to rest them on a pillow if you find your chest falling forward as you meditate.
2. Notice the sounds and sensations of the air moving in and out of your body as you inhale and exhale. Notice the movement of your chest, as it moves up and out as you inhale, and down and in as you exhale.
3. Now shift your focus to just your exhale—the sound of the air as it leaves your body, the feeling of the air as it moves out

of your nose or mouth, the movement of your chest as it moves down and in. You can't help but notice when you are inhaling but all of your attention is on your exhale. Allow yourself to be filled up with and surrounded by the sensations of exhaling, so that there is no room for worry, thinking, remembering, planning.

4. Once you feel relaxed, think of a moment in your life that brings a smile to your lips. One that fills you with happiness and joy or the excitement of being alive. It could be from a simple moment such as sitting in your house when it is quiet and peaceful, looking out at the day beginning and sipping on a warm cup of coffee or receiving a hug from an important person in your life. It could be from a bigger moment in your life such as a birth, receiving news that you were chosen for a job, or creating art that feels just right. Let your Deepest Wisdom guide you to a memory that fills you with joy and Light.

5. Notice not what you are thinking, but how you are feeling within your body as you remember this moment. Can you feel a shift? A feeling of being more solid and grounded? A feeling of quiet inner peace? A feeling of greater love and acceptance for who you are?

6. Sit for a few more minutes with the feeling of safety and love that is filling you. Know that it is there whenever you choose to connect with these memories again.

Living Protected by Our Fear

Every day of our lives, we struggle with fear; fear from life, fear from others, and fear within ourselves. We fear change, being judged and rejected, feeling unimportant, not belonging, etc.—or any of the other Ten Foundational Fears. There are six different ways we respond to feeling these fears.

1. **Negative Emotions and Hurtful Behaviors.** A cascade of Darkness explodes within us whenever we are afraid. Sometimes the explosion is so small we don't even notice it in ourselves and sometimes it is so large, everyone around us feels its reverberations. This explosion begins with fear, grows to include negative emotions, and then expands into hurtful, destructive behaviors that we express towards ourselves and others.

2. **Create expectations.** We create expectations for those we live and work with, so that they can keep us safe. When our expectations are met, we feel less fear. By creating expectations, we also now have a constant nagging fear that the people we are counting on will let us down. We fear that they will not meet our expectations and we will end up feeling afraid, betrayed, disappointed, and hurt.

3. **Restrict who we are.** When the fear comes in the form of expectations from our families, communities, and society, we respond by restricting who we are. We change who, what, and how we are so that others feel safe with us and therefore see us

as acceptable and lovable. The rules about who we are allowed to be as determined by these expectations result in the creation of subconscious beliefs.

4. **Trauma induced limits.** To ensure that we do not re-experience the overwhelming fears that come from traumas, we create extremely limiting subconscious beliefs in which we restrict an aspect of ourself so that we can be safe.

5. **Learn from trusted caregivers.** We have learned and adopted our caregivers' ways of coping with their fears by taking on some of their subconscious beliefs and making them our own.

6. **Learn from Society.** Lastly, we have the subconscious beliefs that we adopted from society's rules so that we fit in with our family and community.

Each of these ways of responding to our fears has added substance to our Suit of Darkness and the threads that hold it together. Each time we respond to fear in one of these six ways, we become even more attached to our suit and convinced of our need for it.

The Lens of Fear

When we feel fear, our subconscious beliefs can act as distortive lenses through which we look at the world, at others, and at ourselves. Each belief blocks, bends, or warps the aspect of reality that does not agree with its view. In this way, we only see a small part of the truth of any situation.

It's a self-validating system. As a result, we live in our own self-imposed world, out of touch with what is truly happening to us and around us. This is especially true when we surround ourselves with others who share our beliefs. This occurs most often with respect to our Societal Beliefs, which are shared within a community, because then we all dismiss and distort reality in exactly the same way. As a group, we believe our take on reality is the only real one because our views are validated by many. We don't recognize how limited our understanding of reality is because everyone around us sees it exactly the same way.

The effect of our subconscious beliefs on our perception of reality makes it impossible for us to see the whole truth. This distortion occurs so quickly and subconsciously we are not aware it is happening. We may honestly believe what we are seeing and interpreting is the truth. We don't see we have altered reality into what we need it to be in order to feel safe.

For example, let's imagine you believe "I don't deserve to be loved." Imagine a friend or member of your family coming up to you and saying, "I love you!," or giving you a hug or a small gift. Now try to imagine what you might think after receiving these demonstrations of love, knowing that deep down inside you believe you are unlovable. You may tell yourself, "They are just trying to be nice," "They are lying," "They want something from me," or "They say that but it means nothing." In seconds, the truth of this person's connection to you and their feelings for you have become empty words and gestures to you. Your belief that you are someone who cannot be loved remains unchallenged. It doesn't matter how many times others express their love for you, you will never believe it! As long as love triggers fear in you and activates the belief that you don't deserve to be loved, this scenario cannot change. Not until you learn to see and release your fears so that they no longer have the power to distort your perspective of the truth.

By disregarding any aspects of reality that feel threatening, we believe we can avoid feeling more fear. The world becomes more predictable and controllable when we live in a world that agrees with what we believe. The truth is that we are unknowingly being controlled by the subconscious beliefs we have adopted and created to help us cope with fear.

The most reliable way to see this process of fear is blocking our understanding of reality, is to notice our emotional attachment to the way we "see" other people, life, the world. The more intense our negative emotions when we imagine thinking, seeing, or believing differently than we currently do, the more likely fear is present and is controlling our perceptions. As we learn the tools to release our fears, we can start to free ourselves of the powerful distorting effects of our subconscious beliefs on our perspective.

Conscious Versus Subconscious

If Our Conscious and Subconscious Beliefs Were in a Fight, the Subconscious Would Always Win

We assume it's our conscious mind that controls how we respond, who we are attracted to, and what choices we make. It can be a shock to learn how powerful our subconscious is and that it has ultimate control over all aspects of our life. Some examples of that control include: those times in life when we sabotage our efforts to obtain what we desire most. The times when we get caught up in patterns that we just keep repeating even though it hurts us. The times when we are responding to people, life, the world just like our caregivers, even though we swore we would never allow that to happen. Since we are unaware of our subconscious beliefs and their impact, it is often only in retrospect we see their profound effects on our lives.

The big question is, what happens when our conscious and subconscious beliefs don't agree. We have conscious ideas, hopes, and dreams of the person we want to be, the life we want to live, and how we want to respond to the injustices of life. Yet these ideals are often in direct conflict with the subconscious beliefs we adopted as small children from our caregivers and society and created from traumas. When dissension occurs between our two sets of beliefs, we may try consciously to choose and believe differently, but ultimately whenever we feel fear, our subconscious beliefs will override any conscious beliefs.

For example, perhaps someone subconsciously believes to be safe when they fear they won't get what they think they want and need, they must be in control of themselves, others, and life. They may have been told they are too controlling by friends and partners and are working on changing it. They may have consciously decided that from now on they will let people control their own lives, and give them space to make their own decisions. This works until they fear they won't get what they think they want and need and in that moment their subconscious beliefs concerning control spring into action. Once that happens, their need to feel safe trumps all their good intentions and they feel overwhelmed with the need to start controlling again. Again and again they may think they are succeeding at changing, only to fail again the moment this fear takes control.

This isn't to say that we can't change. Pitting conscious choices against subconscious beliefs is not going to be the way we can successfully do it. Our subconscious beliefs are only powerful when we are afraid, so when we learn to let go of our fears and connect to our Light, we can choose how we want to be in the world rather than letting our subconscious beliefs choose for us.

Section 4:

The Patterns Created from our Subconscious Belief

Our subconscious beliefs act as our intermediaries with the world. They help us respond to moments in life when we are filled with fear. It could be any of the Ten Foundational Fears such as I'm not enough, or I don't matter, or I'm defective. These fears are triggered into action when we are with others who are afraid, when the world and life is changing in ways we can't control or predict or when something occurs in our life that makes us question our worth. When this happens, our subconscious beliefs tell us how to respond, who to assign blame to, how to understand our involvement, and how to treat ourselves and others. Each of us has a predictable response or pattern as directed by the subconscious beliefs we adopted from our caregivers and family.

Eliora

The Patterns of Blame

In those moments, when a mistake is made or something is wrong, Foundational Fear #1 is triggered within us. (Foundational Fear #1—**Failing**. The fear that we will fail, make mistakes, or get something wrong. Then we will be judged, rejected, and condemned by ourselves and by others.) It doesn't matter if the mistake was our fault or not, this fear is triggered.

To help us cope with this particular fear, we have adopted some of the same subconscious beliefs our caretakers rely on to keep them safe. When we are triggered by this fear, these subconscious beliefs work together to direct how we think, our perspective, and our behavior. As a result, they create a repeatable pattern which we depend on to whenever we feel this fear.

There are three different and predictable patterns that people use when life goes wrong or mistakes are made. They are *mutually exclusive* and each of us goes through life relying on one specific way of responding. It is important to remember that the pattern we respond with is not the result of personal choice. It is determined by the subconscious beliefs we adopted from our families.

The three patterns are:

1. **Blaming-In.** We blame ourselves; it's all our fault. We hold ourselves ultimately responsible even when it is clearly *not* our fault.

2. **Blaming-Out.** We blame anyone but ourselves. We find reasons why it's anyone or anything else's fault, just not our own.
3. **Pretending.** We pretend that there isn't a mistake or problem so there is no reason to get upset or bothered.

Whenever there is a mistake, when someone has gotten it wrong, when the world is wrong, then Foundational Fear #1 is triggered in us and we respond with one of these patterns. People who blame-in believe that they will be safe when they take the responsibility for the mistake. By taking the blame, they are responding as one of their caregivers does to this fear. Likewise, those people who blame-out are directed by the subconscious beliefs they adopted as children to feel safest when they find a reason why the situation is not their fault and to blame out. Lastly, those people who pretend believe at a subconscious level that to even acknowledge there is a problem or mistake is dangerous.

When we are in situations where mistakes have been made, or problems are occurring, our response will remain the same. This is because it's based on our subconscious beliefs which do not change with time. Just as we cannot alter those beliefs, we cannot change the resulting patterns they generate. It is only by learning to release our fears, that we can change this sequence of events.

When we respond to mistakes and problems with these patterns, we benefit by feeling safer because we have a predictable and known way of responding. We benefit by being like our caregivers and families. After all, we learned and adopted these beliefs from them. By sharing their beliefs, we respond with the same patterns as they do. This means we are sharing their way of seeing and responding to the world and life. Behaving similarly to others increases our chances of belonging, being loved, and accepted as one of the group.

Because these patterns are based on fear, when we express them we hurt ourselves and others. Each pattern is triggered by fear and is controlled by our subconscious beliefs that were adopted or created in response to fear, and its purpose is to help us cope with fear. Besides triggering this pattern, the fear also creates Darkness within us in the form of negative emotions, distorted perspective, and hurtful behaviors that we express towards ourselves and others. Because the benefits of feeling safe and belonging are so vital, we continue using these patterns no matter how much pain and suffering they cause.

How often we feel this fear determines how often we live our lives caught up in these patterns. There are some who live their lives constantly triggered by Foundational Fear #1. They go through life on high alert looking for any reasons they might be seen or judged as making a mistake and thus be rejected. As a result, their pattern is their constant companion always directing their thinking, perspective, and behavior. For others, the fear is felt less often, so the pattern is only expressed intermittently when triggering circumstances occur.

Because this response is controlled by our subconscious, we go through life often unaware that this pattern is in response to fear; the fear of being judged and rejected as a failure for making a mistake or getting something wrong. The script for each pattern is already written, our responses already planned out, our thoughts and reactions already occurring often before we even recognize we are afraid.

The Elephant

Of all mammals, the elephant has the longest gestation period, which lasts anywhere between 620 days and 680 days. That's eighteen to twenty-two months, almost two years. Scientists posit that this long gestation period has evolved to ensure the elephant reaches the needed size and the brain capacity to survive. (Unlike humans who are born helpless.) Let's also talk about size. A newborn elephant is about a meter (3.3 feet) tall and weighs about 220 pounds.

Those who have been present at the birth of an elephant say that when the baby emerges and its feet touch the ground, the earth moves.

To anyone present, of all the animals in the kingdom, right from day one, there can be no question of the baby's elephant's significance. They enter the world that way.

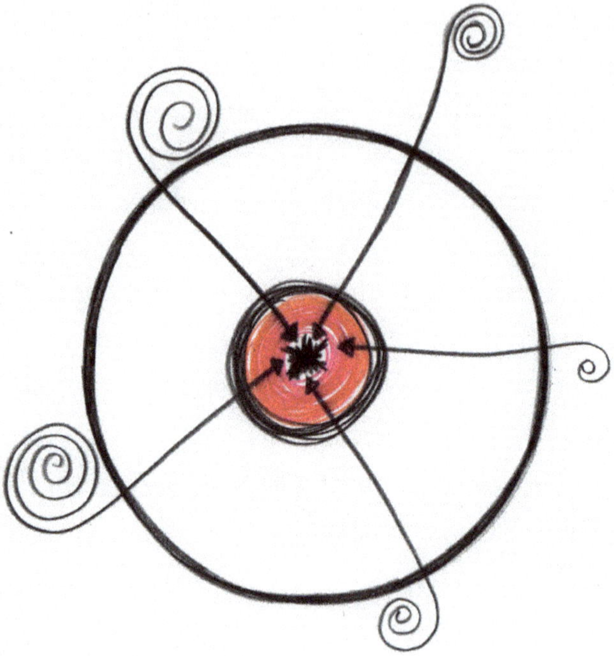

The First Pattern: Blaming-In

Whenever there is a mistake, when someone has gotten it wrong, or when the world is wrong, Foundational Fear #1 is triggered within all of us. This fear then activates those subconscious beliefs created to help keep us safe. As these beliefs take over, they begin to direct how we will respond in this situation. Those who blame in will always find some way to blame themselves no matter what the situation, even when it is clearly not their fault. The key to understanding this pattern is to recognize who they ultimately hold responsible for the mistake or problem. Sometimes, they may appear as if they are trying to find someone else to blame, but inside they are still looking for reasons why it is their fault.

The subconscious beliefs unique to the Blame-In pattern include "To be safe when a mistake was made or something has gone wrong, I must: blame myself, find myself to be at fault, be responsible, and be held responsible." Those people who have these beliefs believe they are safest when can find reasons why they are at fault. It has less to do with the actual circumstances of who made the mistake and more to do with finding some reason to blame themselves so that they can feel safe.

As with all subconscious beliefs, once they are activated, the mind begins to filter all aspects of reality and to only accept those that agree with the beliefs. In the case of those who blame in, their perspective becomes distorted by their beliefs, "To feel

Drink From the Well

safe, whenever I a mistake has been made, I must always be to blame." In this way, any truth that suggests it might be someone else's fault becomes less important than finding a reason to blame themselves. As a result, they may ignore or down play someone else's culpability so they can focus instead on their own blame. Each reason they find to blame themselves helps them feel safer.

At the same time as they blaming themselves to feel safer, the fear they made a mistake and will be judged and rejected has begun to trigger negative emotions in them such as feeling guilty, inadequate, shame, unforgiveable self-hatred, rage, and bitterness. The destructive quality of some of these emotions can be so overwhelming that they need an outlet. Because they blame-in, they will often direct this destructiveness towards themselves. On occasion, however, they may lash out at others. It's important to realize that in this case, hurting others is different from blaming them.

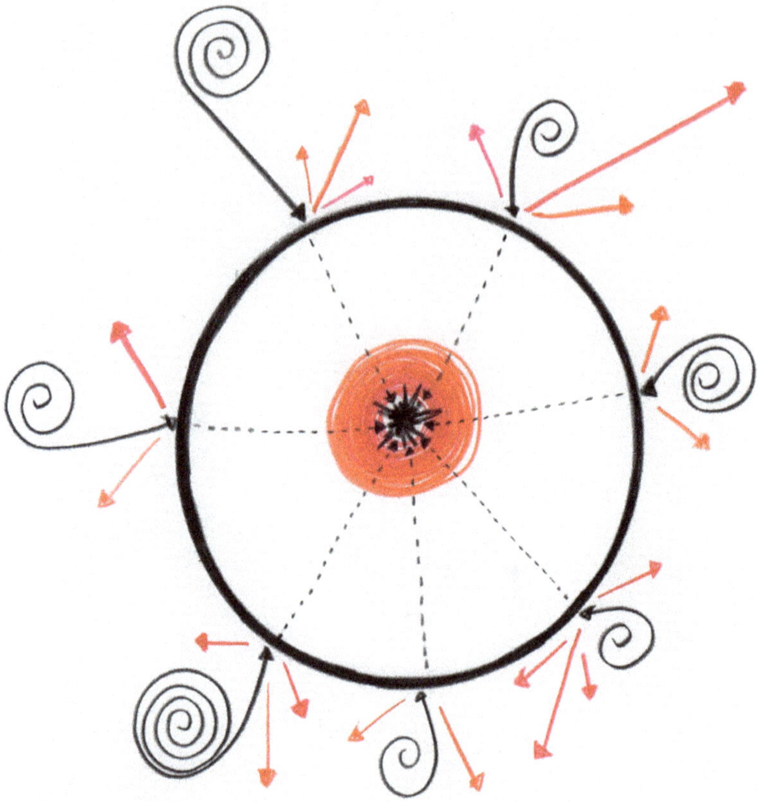

The Second Pattern: Blaming-Out

In situations where mistakes have been made or people have gotten something wrong, people who blame-out will always find reasons to make it someone or something else's fault. The list of who and what they blame is enormous and can include life, the world, fate/luck, the Divine, their mothers and fathers, their Third-grade teachers, the weather, faulty alarm clocks, and pets. They can always find a reason why the responsibility for the mistake or problem lies elsewhere.

What causes all those who respond with this pattern to behave this way are the shared subconscious beliefs: "To stay safe, when a mistake is made, I must always look outward to place blame and make someone else responsible for the mistake." Once a mistake is made and the fear triggered, their subconscious beliefs immediately start to filter reality. For a person who blames-out, their mind focuses only on those aspects of the situation which provides reasons why someone or something else is responsible for the mistake or problem. Any reason they can come up with to blame someone or something else helps them feel safe. This isn't to say they can't take responsibility when it is clearly their fault, but they will always find someone or something else that takes the ultimate responsibility. For example, "If you had warned me there was a red light, I wouldn't have gone through it and gotten a ticket." "If it hadn't gotten windy, then the car's roof rack which I installed would have stayed attached." "If fate hadn't dealt me such a bad hand, then I would have succeeded." It doesn't have to appear logical to the outside world, just plausible to the person who blames-out.

Unfortunately, when people perceive the cause of their problems and mistakes as external, they see themselves as victims. By giving the power and control to others, life, the world, the Divine, they end up feeling used, misused, and unfairly punished by these external forces. As victims, they then see themselves as powerless to achieve the positive change they long to have in their lives. Just because they see themselves as a victim however, doesn't mean they are someone who blames-out. Other Patterns created to respond to different Foundational Fears can also cause people to see themselves as victims.

Like those who blame-in or pretend, when this fear is triggered, it is followed by a cascade of negative emotions and destructive behaviors. In the case of those who blame-out, the common negative emotions are hurt, disappointed, punished, used, mistreated, let down, anger, rage, and resentment. As these emotions grow in intensity, they often lead to lashing out especially at those they believe are at fault.

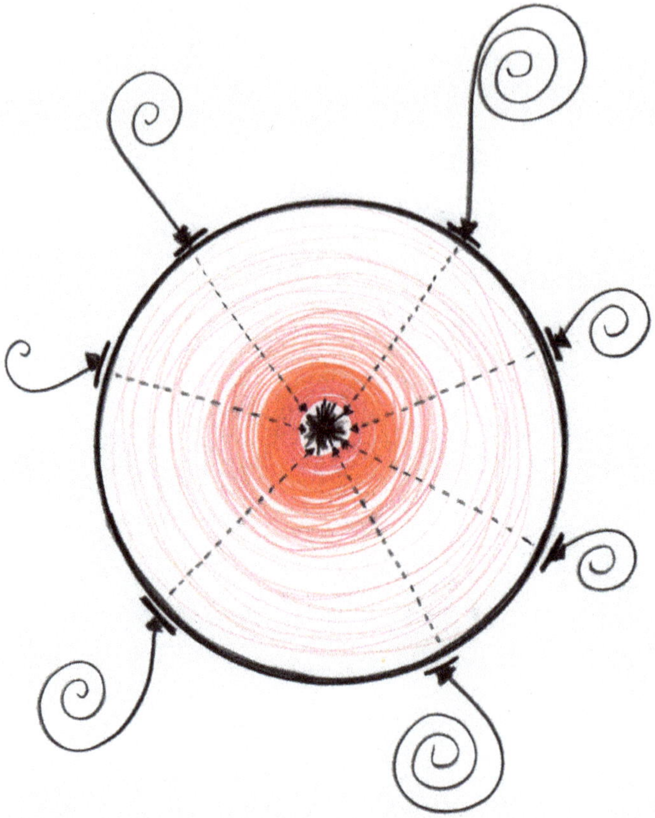

The Third Pattern: The Pretenders

Although most people respond to Foundational Fear #1 by blaming in or out, there are a small percentage of people who do neither. Their subconscious beliefs created in response to this fear direct them to pretend. They do this by playing down the mistake or problem, or refusing to label whatever is occurring as a mistake or problem. In this way, they can avoid blaming and even that there is a reason to feel afraid. By pretending, they can see the situation as one in which there is no mistake or problem, so that it can still be sorted out or modified.

Those with this Pretend pattern have subconscious beliefs such as "To be safe, when Fear # 1 is triggered within me, I must pretend that there are no mistakes or problems." They adopted these particular beliefs from caregivers or family to help them feel safe in response to this fear.

As soon as they feel this fear, their subconscious beliefs are activated and their Pretend pattern takes control. They often don't even have a chance to notice there is a mistake or problem before their beliefs are controlling their perspective on the situation. By not seeing the mistakes and problems, their subconscious is helping them to feel safe. It's important to note that this particular pattern is in response to Foundational Fear #1 and that there are other pretend patterns created in response to other Foundational Fears.

Even as people with this pattern pretend there is no problem or mistake, the fear that they made a mistake or gotten it wrong is still triggered within them. As they feel this fear, the emotional response starts to build within them and it pushes to be expressed. Because it's unclear why these Dark emotions and behaviors are appearing, they do not understand the cause of their response. They may be feeling negative emotions such as hurt, anxious, used, anger, punished, and resentful. Just as with the other patterns they may feel the need to hurt themselves or others with their words or behavior, as an outlet for these emotions. Unlike the other patterns, though, they won't see the clear relationship between the situation that triggered the response and their negative emotions and behaviors.

What Happens to These Patterns When Fear is No Longer Present?

As we learn to recognize and release the fears that trigger our subconscious beliefs, and the patterns they control, we begin to have a choice of how we want to act rather than reacting. We will no longer be overwhelmed with the negative emotions and hurtful behaviors that the fear induces in us. We will no longer need to blame or pretend, instead we can choose the best way to deal with the situation for ourselves and everyone else from a place of clarity and peace rather than fear and defensiveness.

Tools to Connect: Which Blame Pattern Do You Have?

Sometimes we believe we know how we respond when mistakes have been made, other times its less clear. This tool will help you take the time to notice exactly how you respond when mistakes are made, by you and by others. As you remember such moments from your life, you will get greater understanding of what your pattern responses actually look and feel like.

As a quick review, people who blame-in respond to mistakes by blaming themselves even when it is obvious they are not responsible. A person with this pattern will always find some way to hold themselves ultimately responsible for someone else's error or even just bad luck. A person with the blame-out response will always find some person or thing to blame even if it is clearly their fault. They may agree they made a mistake but the ultimate responsibility will always be assigned to an external person or factor. A person with the pretending pattern will ignore there is a problem or mistake. They will pretend either there is no problem at all or that it's unimportant and doesn't upset them in the least.

A Meditation to Help You Identify Your Pattern

1. Sit as tall as is comfortable, with your chest up and open. Partially or completely close your eyes. Rest your hands in your lap with your palms up and open. It can be helpful to rest them on a pillow if you find your chest falling forward as you meditate.
2. Notice the sounds and sensations of the air moving in and out of your body as you inhale and exhale. Notice the movement of your chest, as it moves up and out as you inhale, and down and in as you exhale.
3. Now shift your focus to just your exhale—the sound of the air as it leaves your body, the feeling of the air as it moves out of your nose or mouth, the movement of your chest as it moves down and in. You can't help but notice when you are inhaling but all of your attention is on your exhale. Allow yourself to be filled up with and surrounded by the sensations of exhaling, so that there is no room for worry, thinking, remembering, planning.
4. When you feel relaxed and peaceful, remember a moment in which you clearly made a mistake or got something wrong. If that feels impossible, remember a moment when those around you were upset about mistakes being made. It could be from yesterday or twenty years ago, it doesn't matter.
5. As you relive the memory, how did you respond? What were you feeling? What were your thoughts? What were you saying to yourself, or to others? How were you behaving towards

yourself or others? Note it down, so that you can capture the details of the experience.

6. Now allow yourself to remember another time in your life when a mistake was made that was clearly <u>not</u> your fault. If that feels impossible, remember a moment when those around you were upset about mistakes being made. Notice how you responded to this memory. What were your feelings, thoughts, reactions, and your behaviors? What were you saying to yourself or others? How were you treating yourself or others? Note down the details of this time as well.

7. Are you seeing a pattern in how you respond to this fear? If it's unclear, you may need to ask who did you ultimately blame for the mistake. Ultimately is the key word here. For a person that Blames-In, they may acknowledge that someone else made the mistake but still blame themselves for perhaps not stopping them from doing it. For a person who Blames-Out, they may agree they made the mistake but still be looking for something or someone else to ultimately be held responsible for the mistake to occur, such as bad luck, the weather, their upbringing, etc. If it's unclear, take the time to meditate as you remember more times when mistakes were made or people got things wrong, and noticing how you responded in each instance. If you are struggling to remember moments in your life when mistakes were made, it could be the result of having a Pretending pattern. For those of you with this pattern, your subconscious beliefs

will prevent you from seeing or acknowledging there is or was a mistake or problem. This difficulty remembering such moments can help you see how your Pretending pattern is protecting you from even recognizing or accepting mistakes or problems are occurring.

Four More Patterns: "The Best of the Best," "Wallflower," "Mr. or Ms. Right," or "Fake It 'Til You Make It"

We have multiple patterns to help us cope with each of the Foundational Fears. The Blaming patterns were created to help us respond to Foundational Fear #1. This second set of 4 patterns were created to help us cope with Foundational Fear #6. (Foundational Fear #6—**Worthless**. The fear that who we are deep down inside is a monster. We fear that we are nothing or a nobody or that we are broken and defective. We fear that we are a worthless, useless, unlovable, unlikable, or undesirable person.).

There are 4 patterns in this set and each is the product of the subconscious beliefs we adopted and created in response to fearing we are worthless or that others see us that way. Because our patterns are based on the subconscious beliefs, we adopt from our caregivers, we have absolutely no choice which pattern we manifest.

The four patterns triggered by this fear are called "The Best of the Best," "Wallflowers," "Mr. or Ms. Right," and "Fake It 'Til You Make It." Each of the four patterns have two primary goals. The first is to help us to feel safe when we fear we are worthless. The second is to prevent others from seeing us as worthless and judging and rejecting us. Each pattern relies on the creation of a unique façade to stop others and sometimes even ourselves from seeing ourselves as broken, defective, worthless, unlovable, etc.

When you read the descriptions, you might recognize yourself in one or more of the patterns, but you have only one true pattern. Your true pattern is determined by your behavior only when you are genuinely afraid that you are worthless, or others see and judge you this way. This fear must be present for the pattern and its subconscious beliefs to be triggered into activity. Without this fear, the pattern is not apparent.

It can sometimes be quite challenging to identify our pattern or other people's patterns. This is because we look at the overall behavior of the person, not just their behavior when they are filled with the fear that they are worthless. As we grow up in households with caretakers who have patterns different from our own, we sometimes mimic their behavior. Just because we share some of the behaviors with a pattern, however, doesn't mean we respond with this pattern when we are afraid. This is because we haven't adopted the underlying subconscious beliefs responsible for their pattern, we have merely learned to behave as they do. As a result, these learned behaviors can occur anytime in the presence and absence of the fear, but our true pattern only occurs when Foundational Fear #6 is present.

When we fear we are worthless or that others will judge us this way, our subconscious immediately responds by activating those beliefs that were created to keep us safe from this fear. Our subconscious beliefs take control by filtering the reality of the world around us. Our pattern's protective facades are created from our skewed perspectives of reality.

The role of each façade is to convince others that this fear is not true and we aren't worthless. Depending on our pattern, the façade can be used to convince ourselves, as well, that we have value. This façade works by changing how we see ourselves, others, and the world. Sometimes this façade just plays out in our minds and we think we are the best, right, invisible, or exactly who we should be and sometimes we need to say it out loud so we can convince ourselves and all those present we are not worthless. For some people, their façade is so successful they even believe it is true.

As our subconscious beliefs and thus our patterns begin to take control and direct our thoughts, and perspective, the underlying fear is simultaneously triggering a cascade of negative emotions and destructive behaviors. This Dark response adds a hurtful and destructive element to each pattern as it is being expressed.

A person with this pattern only expresses it when they are afraid, they are worthless, or others see and judge them this way. Since we constantly face external expectations and judgement from others, life, and the world, we often feel this fear. As a result, many of us define ourselves by our pattern when we think of who we are and how we are in the world.

Because our response to this fear is controlled by our subconscious, we are not aware it is happening. It is easier for those around us to see the changes in us when the pattern takes control than to see it in ourselves. Often the only thing we notice is that suddenly we are becoming defensive and at the same time we are beginning to feel negative emotions and behave in hurtful ways to ourselves and/or others. We have learned to rely on this pattern to help us feel safe in a scary, judgmental, and rejecting world. These patterns and their underlying subconscious beliefs are major component of the Suit of Darkness that we created to help us avoid more fear.

Faith

I saw a greeting card at the grocery store last week. The front bore an illustration of a comet shooting through the sky. Underneath was a quotation by Sojourner Truth:

I'm not going to die. I'm going home like a shooting star.

Once home, I dropped the groceries on my kitchen counter, leaving ice cream melting in the bag.

I walked the streets near my house directionless, looking up, until it was dark.

How would it feel to say something like that, so certain in your faith you were made fearless?

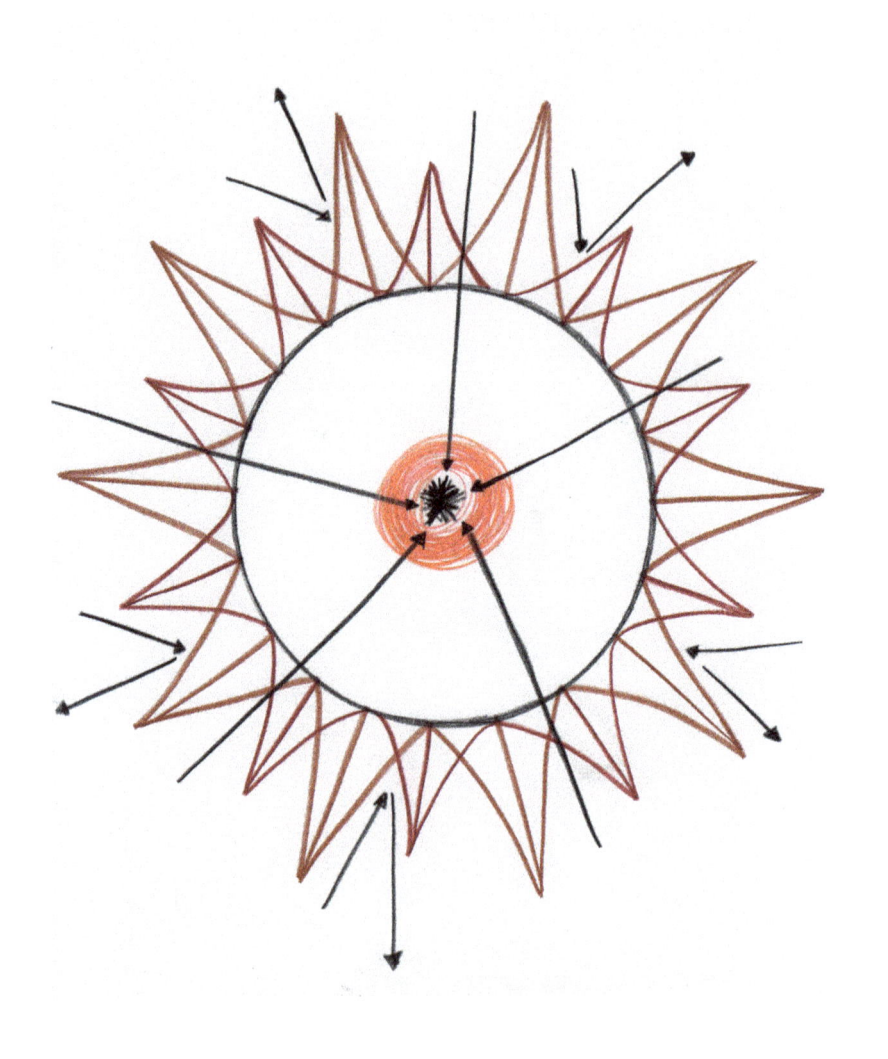

Eliora

Pattern One: The Best of the Best

The first of the four patterns is "The Best of the Best." For those who express this pattern, there is only one way they believe they can be safe from the fear they are worthless, and that is to convince themselves and everyone else that they are "the best". This pattern's subconscious beliefs include, "To stay safe when I fear I am worthless or others will see and judge me that way, I must always be the best of the best, the most adored, the most successful, the most intelligent, etc." This is not to say that everyone with this pattern is successful in life or widely admired. The point here is simply to describe the edges and walls of this pattern so you can understand its composition. What people do with these beliefs and how they live their lives is different for each person and is based on their life experiences, personality, and abilities.

The beliefs and the pattern people create protect them from this fear by building a façade designed to convince themselves and others that this fear could not possibly be true because they are so clearly superior to most other people. Some people with this pattern need to see themselves as the best in one or two aspects of their lives. Others need to be the best in every aspect of who they are.

As with all subconscious beliefs triggered by fear, these beliefs immediately begin to filter the reality of the world. In the case of people with this pattern, they begin to focus on those aspects of reality that support their belief that they are the best and to ignore those aspects that suggest otherwise. This distorted perspective ultimately controls how they are allowed to think, respond, and behave.

To convince themselves they are the best, they are often on the lookout for those they see as inferior and to whom they can compare themselves. Depending on how afraid they are that they are worthless, people with this pattern may feel protected from the fear, just noting their superiority in their minds. Other times they may need to dismiss, ridicule, and put down the other person to convince themselves and other that they are the best.

Each of these coping patterns creates vicious cycles that make them challenging to escape once they have been triggered by fear. In the case of "The Best of the Best," to live their life no longer controlled by this fear means that they are also letting go of the protective perspective provided by the pattern that they are the best. They may fear that unless they remain vigilant and are "The Best," they will not be safe from being judged as worthless. After all, it's a huge drop from The Best all the way down to Nothing Special. The fear of this status change causes those with this pattern to cling to it even more strongly. The only way someone caught up in this pattern can escape it is to learn to recognize and acknowledge the underlying fear that triggers it. Looking objectively at our fears reduces their ability to trigger our subconscious beliefs and thus our patterns.

As is true with all patterns, when people who have the "Best of the Best" pattern are not afraid of seeing themselves or being judged by others as worthless, defective, unlovable, etc. they can relax and enjoy being themselves. They feel safe accepting and valuing themselves and those around them.

Questions

A group of students were devoted to a teacher they adored. Without charge, he met them every day near the fountain and answered all their questions and taught them what he knew. One day they rushed into the temple agitated and yelling.

"Master, today on the way to you, we saw a man kicking his dog in the street."

"It was horrible," another said.

"What a terrible person," they wailed.

"He should be locked up."

The guru waited until they were quiet. "You'll be enlightened when you feel as badly for the man as you do for the dog."

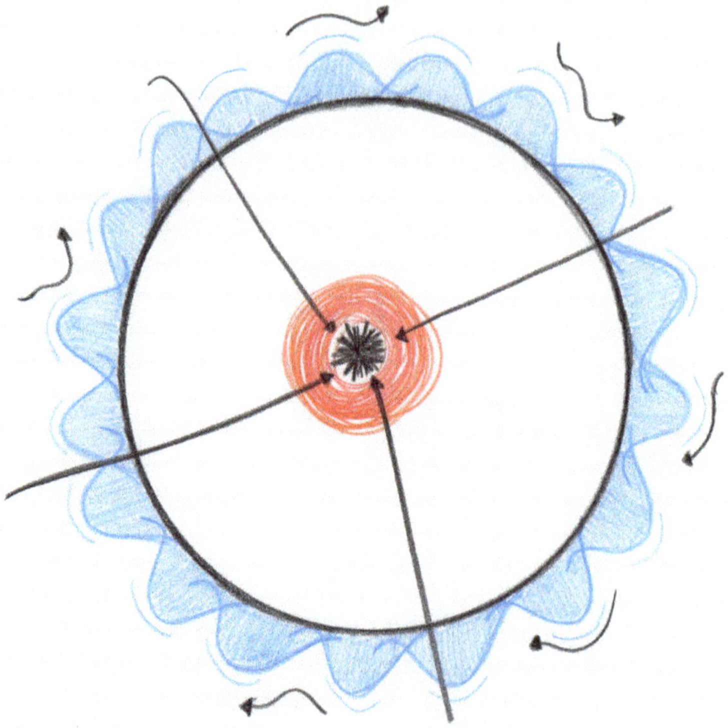

Pattern Two: Wallflowers

The next pattern is called "Wallflower" because in the presence of the fear they are worthless, this pattern directs the person to try to become invisible, to hide in plain sight. The "Wallflower's" protective wall is quite different from those of the other three patterns, whose protective façade casts them in a positive light as superior, right, or exactly the person they should be. For the "Wallflower," there is no pretending this fear doesn't exist or doesn't apply to them. There is only a protective façade that cries, "Please don't see me! Don't look at me!" In this way the "Wallflowers" hope by being invisible, no one will see the truth, that there is a very good chance they are worthless. Their subconscious beliefs include "To be safe, when I fear I am worthless is to hide or be judged as worthless." "To be safe, I must become invisible, for I fear that I am worthless, and others may see me that way."

A "Wallflower" pattern is difficult to dismantle once they are caught up in it. As soon as they feel fear, their mind distorts any aspect of reality that suggests it is safe to be seen and known by others. They can only see aspects of reality that agree with their belief it is safer to hide in the face of fear. In hiding, they feel increasingly unsafe and unworthy. It can become a vicious cycle of feeling fear and hiding, then feeling even more fear. The only way to break the cycle is to learn to see the triggering fear and to let it go so that the subconscious beliefs and the pattern are no longer activated and expressed.

Like "The Best of the Best," the "Wallflower's" pattern is only present and active when they are triggered to feel Foundational Fear #6. However, when they are connected to their Light, feeling safe and loved, this pattern is nowhere in sight. They feel comfortable being known, engaging with others, living life, and being present in the world. The key to knowing if you possess the "Wallflower" pattern is not through general behavior, but how you respond when you are faced with the true fear of worthlessness.

Blue Lotus

If you get lost, seek out the blue lotus.
It lives beneath the tallest trees in the forest—
The oldest ones with the curlicue roots that speak tree to tree,
Underground.

Don't try to research it—
The blue lotus is not found in any book.
It will not allow itself to be photographed.
In fact, it can only be seen by starlight,
Between the whisper of leaves.

You may not approach the blue lotus straight on.
Only with reverence, with soft steps, with a heart open
Or your fear will snap its petals shut and make it seem
To camouflage into the black earth.

When you find it, pull a petal,
Cup it with your fingers
Fill it with clean water
Drink.
Drink more.
Become who you were always meant to be.

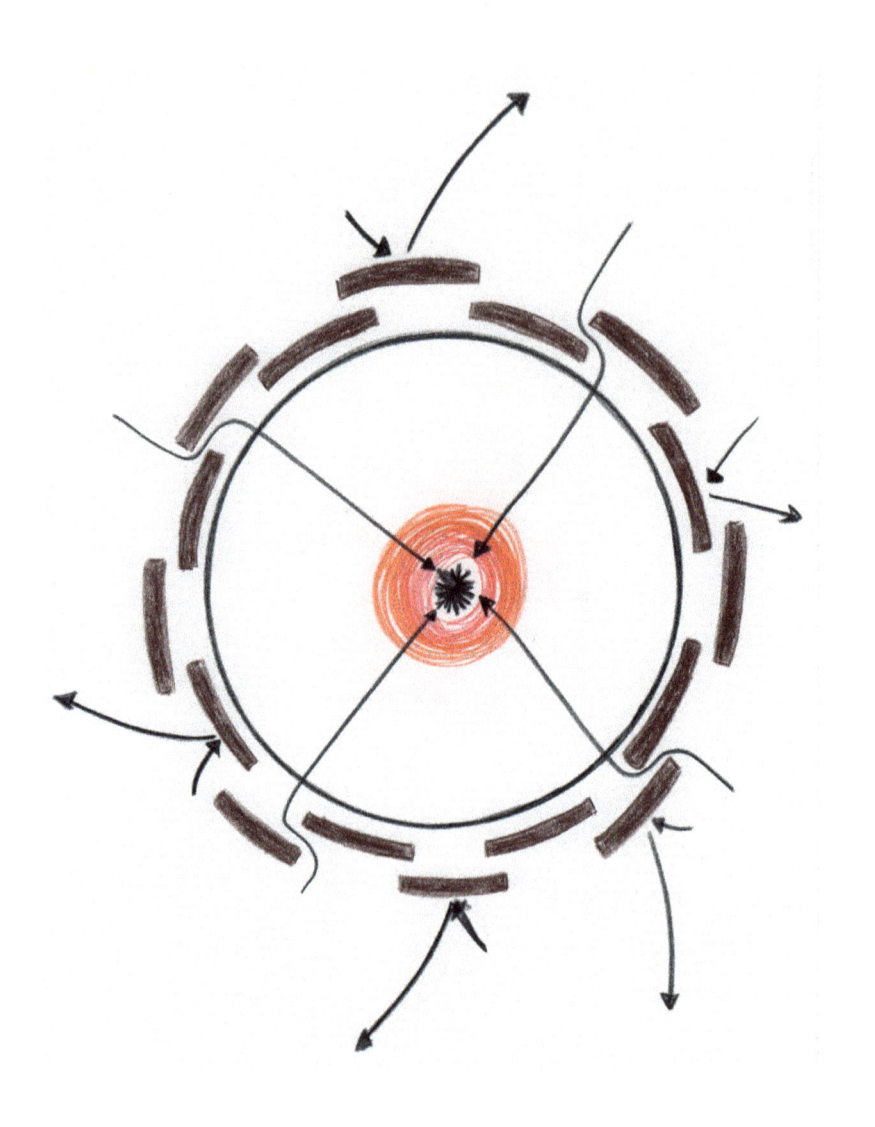

Eliora

Pattern Three: Mr. or Ms. Right

The third pattern is called "Mr. or Ms. Right." When individuals with this pattern fear they are worthless or about to be judged that way by others, they protect themselves by believing they are right, which often means believing they are more knowledgeable and better prepared than everyone else. In moments of fear, they need to see themselves as someone who is always "in the know." They don't need to see themselves or be seen as "The Best of the Best," instead they simply need others to admire them for being right.

Their subconscious beliefs all center around the following belief: "To be safe, when I fear I am worthless or others will see and judge me that way, I must always be right; I must be prepared so that I am right; I must know more than others so that I am right." These beliefs are all variations upon the theme that "to be right" and "to be seen as right" will make them safe.

When these beliefs are triggered by Foundational Fear #6, the subconscious beliefs created in response to that fear begin to take control. Their mind begins to distort and to focus on only those moments when their answers are right, their knowledge is right, they are right and as a result they ignore when others are right or when they were wrong. As they misinterpret reality, they begin to respond and behave in ways that are directed by those misunderstandings. They become entrenched in being right. They may begin to feel resentful and threatened by any right answer that is not their own. They may feel deprived and mistreated when others don't agree with their answers. This may close their mind to learning from others, especially those whose views or opinions they believe are not as right as their own.

This need to be right to prove their worth can make it challenging to extricate themselves from this vicious cycle. The more worthless, broken, unlovable, etc. they fear they are, the greater their need to be right which in turn creates an even greater need to be right and so it goes. There is only one way to break the cycle and that is to take back control from their fears. By learning to release their fears as they occur, the subconscious beliefs and the pattern they trigger will no longer be needed or expressed.

As with the other patterns, when a person with the "Mr. or Ms. Right" pattern is not triggered to feel Foundational Fear #6, their pattern is not in control of their thoughts, perspective, and behavior. They can stop hiding behind their "I'm always right" façade and relax and let go of their need to perform. They are open to learning from others, even those they may have judged as less right and knowledgeable when they were caught up in their fear and thus their pattern.

To Connect to the Divine: Choose One of the Best Memories of Your Life

It doesn't have to be a "big deal" moment. I'm on the west side of the city. I'm there for a meeting about a job. I have hours before the meeting, free to do whatever I want. I'm wearing a red blouse; the sun is shining. I walk into an art store. The walls are filled with turquoise journals, pens of every gemstone color, markers, pastels, thick fibrous paper, paint brushes so tall they reach my knees. I allow myself to buy a sketchbook, a hardcover one with hand binding. My fingers itch to rip it open, to offer myself up, to see what comes out onto those white, blank pages.

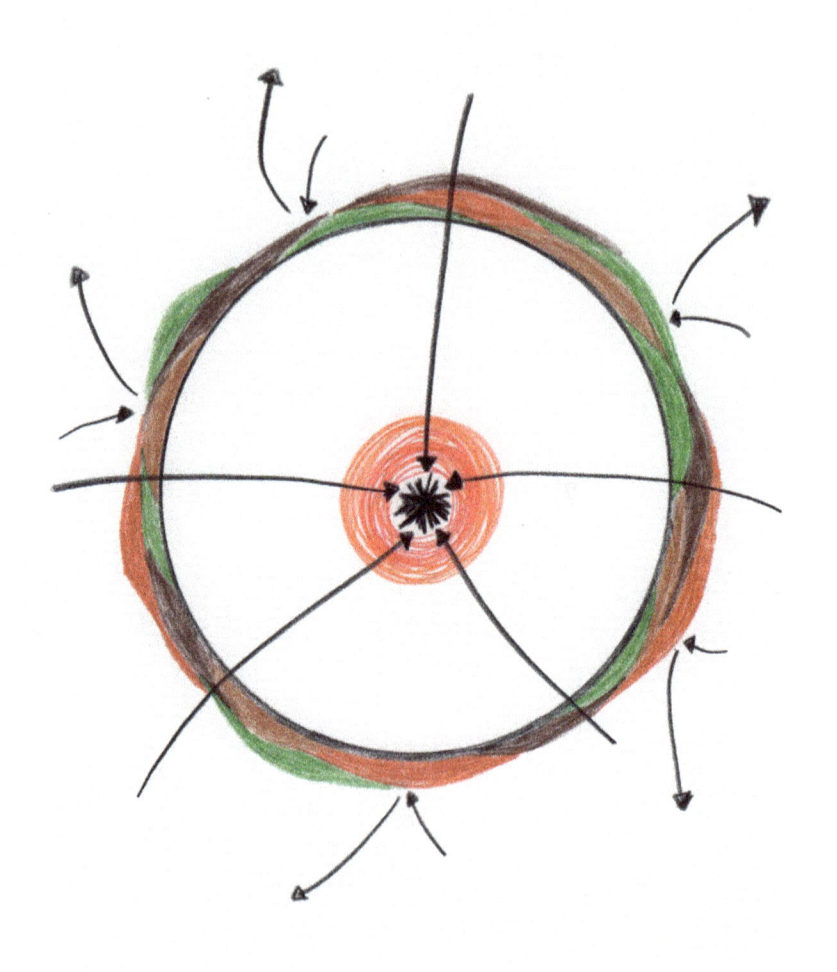

Eliora

Pattern Four: "Fake It 'Til You Make It"

The fourth pattern is "Fake It 'Til You Make It". When people with this pattern are afraid of being judged worthless, they protect themselves by pretending to be the person they "should" be. All of us have a list of "shoulds" learned from our caregivers, families, and society. For people with this pattern, however, their should list takes on added importance. It becomes the basis for the façade they hide behind when Foundational Fear #6 is triggered in them. The subconscious beliefs that trigger this pattern include the following, "To be safe, when I fear I am worthless or that others will see and judge me that way, I must pretend to be the person others expect me to be; the person I "should" be; the person others believe I "should" be."

The Fake It 'Til You Make It pattern can sometimes be confused with "The Best of the Best" pattern as both can drive people towards overachievement. However, the underlying reason for achieving is quite different between the two. The people with Fake It 'Til You Make It focus on achieving as theyy try desperately to fulfill their "should" list. To feel safe, they pretend to be the person others expect of them. They don't need to be "the best," they just need to live up to the expectations of others. On the other hand, "The Best of the Best" people must see themselves and convince others that they are "the best" and will sometimes need to compare and put down those they see as inferior to convince themselves and others this is true.

Drink From the Well

When people with the Fake It Til You Make It group look into the mirror, they see someone who is being a "good" person and living up to their parents', partner's, children's, co-workers'... expectations.

Living with this pattern can create a downward spiral that is challenging to escape. The very façade that keeps a Fake It 'Til You Make It safe is based on pretending, which when it works, can make it difficult for the person to see who they truly are underneath. There is the added fear that if they stop pretending, they will upset others by not living up to their expectations. The only way to break out of this pattern of pretending is to learn to recognize your fear of feeling worthless and others seeing and judging you that way and to let it go. In this way, the subconscious beliefs and the resulting patterns are no longer activated and expressed.

When a person with this pattern Fake It 'Til You Make It is not filled with fear, they can begin to feel safe, loved, and trust they belong, and they can finally let go of their "should" list. They can relax and live their lives as the person they were born with no lingering "shoulds" hanging over their heads.

Where This Information Gets Us

When we can see ourselves caught up in our pattern, we immediately understand that this is who we have learned to be, it isn't who we truly are. There is a sense of relief seeing this truth. As we continue to observe ourselves getting caught up in our pattern, we begin to hear its script playing out in our heads. We learn to feel when the pattern first begins to kick in, and then take over controlling us: our thoughts, words, and actions. We begin to notice when we are responding from the pattern and when we are truly being ourselves. This understanding is an essential first step to liberating ourselves from living controlled by our fears and thus our negative emotions, behaviors, and patterns.

Reading about the patterns and becoming familiar with their facades can help us understand when our friends, family, and acquaintances are overwhelmed with fearing they are worthless. We can see the Wallflower take over when a friend is struggling with work and suddenly becomes invisible whenever you try to connect. We can see the Best of the Best in a new neighbor who boasts about: how everyone loves them, or how rich and powerful they are. We can see Mr. or Ms. Right in a cousin who is trying to find their place in the world and who insists their opinions are right and should be admired. Lastly, we can see Fake-it-til-you-make-it in your co-worker, who is always working so hard on being who others think they "should" be at the expense of their health, happiness, and quality of life. As you begin to indefinity these patterns in friends and family, you can begin to have some compassion for them when they are caught up in their patterns because you now understand how powerful and controlling our fears and patterns can be.

Tools to Connect: Which of the four patterns do you have?

Now that you have read about the four patterns, you may be sure which one you have or you may be mulling between two or three of them. The first step to identify which pattern you use to protect yourself from the seeing yourself or being seen by others as worthless, is to remember how you responded to specific moments in your life when you felt this fear. Because it is only in those moments your pattern will become apparent.

Looking at your behavior when you are not afraid only adds confusion to the identification process. This is because many of us grew up in a households with other patterns in addition to your own. When you were small, you watched your family respond when they were afraid and get caught up in their patterns. As you observed them respond to this fear, you sometimes adopted their subconscious beliefs which are the basis for their pattern and now your pattern. Sometimes you merely copied their behavior as they were expressing their pattern. For example, imagine you are a "Wallflower" but grew up with a caregiver with the "Mr. or Ms. Right" pattern. You learned through observation that this individual has all the answers and thinks they are always right. At some point, you decided that this way of being is admirable. Soon, you became the person others ask for answers, the person who always thinks they are right. You find yourself reading to learn as much as you

Drink From the Well

can, so you are prepared with the answers to questions. What is important to notice, however, is that when you are triggered by feeling worthless, you don't adopt a "Mr. or Ms. Right" pattern, instead you become a "Wallflower," hiding and being invisible. Fear isn't driving you to be right, it's driving you to become invisible.

As a reminder, a person with Pattern One (The Best of the Best) responds to Foundational Fear #6, by ensuring that they and others see them as the best in a few or all aspects of their life. This pattern may dismiss and demean others they see as inferior to ensure others realize they are superior. People with Pattern Two (the Wallflower) respond to this fear by becoming invisible, hidden, and disconnected in the hope that no one sees them and judges them as worthless, or defective. Pattern Three (Mr. or Ms. Right) individuals respond by believing they are always right. Their goal is to be respected and admired as the person who has the right information. Lastly, Pattern Four individuals (Fake It 'Til You Make It) react to this fear by pretending to be the person described in their personal "should" list—brighter and better than any human can possibly be.

<u>A Meditation to Help You Identify Your Pattern</u>

1. Sit as tall as is comfortable, with your chest up and open. Partially or completely close your eyes. Rest your hands in your

lap with your palms up and open. It can be helpful to rest them on a pillow if you find your chest falling forward as you meditate.

2. Notice the sounds and sensations of the air moving in and out of your body as you inhale and exhale. Notice the movement of your chest, as it moves up and out as you inhale, and down and in as you exhale.

3. Now shift your focus to just your exhale—the sound of the air as it leaves your body, the feeling of the air as it moves out of your nose or mouth, the movement of your chest as it moves down and in. You can't help but notice when you are inhaling but all of your attention is on your exhale. Allow yourself to be filled up with and surrounded by the sensations of exhaling, so that there is no room for worry, thinking, remembering, planning.

4. When you feel relaxed and at peace in your body, think of a moment in which you were very afraid that you were worthless, useless, unlovable, defective, or even worse, a monster. It could have been you judging yourself this way or it could be coming from someone else. It doesn't matter if it happened yesterday or twenty years ago.

5. From this calm and relaxed place as you focus on your exhale, relive this moment. Notice your response: what were your feelings, thoughts, reactions, and your behaviors? What were you saying to yourself or others? How were you treating yourself or others?

6. Now remember another moment when you feared you were worthless, unlovable, defective or a monster, in your life. Notice how you were responding to this moment and whether it differs. What were your feelings, thoughts, reactions, and your behaviors? What were you saying to yourself or others? How were you treating yourself or others?

7. Are you seeing a pattern in how you respond to this particular fear? Take the time to focus on your exhale and remember more of these moments, noticing how you responded in each instance.

8. Sometimes, it can seem impossible to identify our pattern, often because we are afraid of seeing and knowing the answer. If you are struggling, step back and stop looking at this time. Knowing these four ways of responding opens you up to new insight into the attitudes and behaviors of others when they are afraid. Over time, this understanding will broaden to include yourself as well.

Section 5

The Darkness that Comes from Fear

All Negative Emotions Come from Fear

Our anger, hurt, hate, grief, resentment, and shame, all the negative emotions we have felt over the course of our life, all are the result of being afraid. Whenever you have felt sad, deep down inside there is fear behind that sadness. Whenever you have felt hate, its fear that caused that hate. The Ten Foundational Fears cover all the aspects of what we fear most in ourselves, relationships, and life. They are the source of all the negative emotions we have experienced in our lifetime.

Fear ⟶ Primary Emotions ⟶ Secondary Emotions

Such as: Hurt	Such As: Anger
Disappointed	Rage
Rejected	Hate
Used	Bitterness
Hopeless	Resentment
Unloved	Frustration
…	…

When we are afraid but don't recognize and acknowledge the fear, a cascade of negative emotions results. There are two different sets of emotions that come from that fear. The first set which are triggered directly from fear are referred to as

Drink From the Well

Primary Emotions. These include the majority of our negative emotions: hurt, unloved, grief, disappointed, abandoned, used, rejected, etc. The second set that are triggered from the Primary Emotions are called the Secondary Emotions. The Primary emotions are triggered when the fear is ignored or repressed and a stronger, more noticeable emotional response is needed to get our attention. The last and final set, the Secondary Emotions are intense, reactive, and destructive. Once we feel these emotions, they are hard to pretend that a fear response is not in progress. The list of Secondary Emotions is much shorter because it is limited only to those emotions that are not directly triggered from fear. They include anger, rage, fury, hate, bitterness, frustration, resentment, aggravation, and other emotions of this nature. When we feel any of these emotions, its accompanied by a desire to hurt, punish, or destroy, although we may never follow through on those fantasies. From that single initial emotion of fear, a cascade of emotions has been released in order to force us to recognize that fear is present and we need to pay attention to it.

Darkness and Light

There are two brothers. Identical twins, striking boys with blue eyes and black hair. Their mother died early, and the father drank and raged and beat them with belts and with the flat side of his hand.

Ten years after they were grown, a news station decided to do a story on the brothers. One was in a halfway house outside Philadelphia, always on and off heroin. The other had created an organization that brought medical aid and eyeglasses to children in countries around the world.

A journalist asked the first brother in the grey halfway house how he ended up there. "My father drank and beat me. My mother died. What else could I do?"

The journalist flew to Portland. She interviewed the other brother in the factory from which they shipped the supplies. She asked this brother how he created an empire, how he was able to help so many children. "My father drank and beat me. My mother died. What else could I do?"

Living with Negative Emotions

As we go through our day, our week, our lives, we assume our negative emotions are a necessary and normal component. We believe that we are destined to feel these emotions and to allow them to control us. The decisions we make or don't make are controlled in large part by how we are feeling. We make decisions about whether we will join in or try something new depending on how anxious we feel. We may let loose with hurtful words and attack ourselves or others when we are angry or filled with rage. We may shut down and retreat from the world, when we are overwhelmed with sadness or grief. Stop for a moment and think back to the last time you felt angry, how did it affect your choices, your speech, your behavior? How about when you were nervous and anxious, how did they affect you? Living our lives controlled by our emotions seems like such a familiar and essential part of our life, it's hard to imagine living any other way.

We learn from our families and society how to live with our negative emotions, use them to our advantage, and "work" through them. Unfortunately, no one ever teaches us how to let them go so that we can be truly free of them. We learn instead that we need to cling to our negative emotions to keep us safe. Think about grudges. When we are holding onto a grudge, we are reliving the negative emotions we experienced—the hurt, disappointment, rage, and hate, to make sure we don't forget them or allow them to diminish in intensity. We believe if we feed the grudge and make it bigger and stronger, we will be protected from being hurt again by the same person or someone like them.

We are taught that to "work" through our emotions, we need to rehash the upset, the outrage, the problem over and over again. We do this by either talking about it with friends or family or by sitting alone and reliving every moment in our minds. Each time we relive the story, our emotions become bigger. Our attachment to the story has become stronger. Rather than helping us let go of our negative emotions, repeating the story, reliving the memory creates more lasting attachment to both the emotions and the story.

Lastly, we mistakenly believe that to let go of our emotions we must fully express them, especially our punitive Secondary Emotions, such as anger, hate, frustration, etc. We do that by venting them directly at ourselves or others by demeaning, labeling, attacking, or abusing. We may also express them more indirectly by undermining, manipulating, and gaslighting. Unfortunately, unleashing our emotions only exacerbates fear and pain. It increases the Darkness within you and spreads it from you to everyone around you.

How to Cope with Our Emotions

The negative emotions accumulated over our lifetime adversely affect us, our lives, and our relationships. For example, every time we are reminded of a grudge that we are holding on to, waves of negative emotion fill us. When we meet someone who reminds us of a hurtful person from our past, those negative emotions contaminate our current emotions, thoughts, and responses. Every time we remember painful or shameful moments from our past, the negative emotions fill and overwhelm us once more. This list of examples is inexhaustible. Our accumulated negative emotions adversely affect almost every aspect of our lives. The problem is we don't know how to recognize these emotions once they are triggered and to let them go.

Feeling our negative emotions can be uncomfortable, overwhelming, and sometimes painful. As a result, we panic and try to get rid of them by repressing or ignoring them. Often when that doesn't work, we try to release them by expressing them: yelling, crying, guilting, blaming, shaming, etc. Unfortunately, none of these techniques work. We may believe we are rid of these emotions, but they are all still with us.

As we go through life, we have been deceived into thinking that being controlled by our negative emotions is inevitable and obligatory. As humans, we excel at adapting to even disagreeable and unpleasant states of existence. We are resigned to our current state of letting our emotions control us rather than us controlling them. Here is a tool to help you work through your negative emotions and to release them.

Releasing Your Emotions

What can we do with all of our negative emotions when there is seemingly no way to let them go? Luckily for us, there is a tool that is easy to use and can help us release any negative emotions we are feeling or have felt. Can you imagine, a tool to help you let go of the anxiety, anger, grief, hate, all the negative emotions accumulated in your lifetime? Can you imagine no longer needing to lash out, punish, hurt, blame, or shame anyone because you are overwhelmed with negative emotions and don't know how to cope with them? By learning to release your negative emotions, you can now take responsibility for them. You no longer need to take them out on anyone else as you try to "work" through them.

Riding the Waves of Our Emotions to Release Them

The basis of this tool is learning to connect with our emotions in a new way that feels less overwhelming and scary than drowning in their intensity and pain as we relive the memory and the waves of emotions fill us. There are two ways we experience our emotions: mentally and physically. This is because each emotion creates physical sensations in our bodies when they are being expressed. Think of a moment when you were filled with grief or sadness. Where did you feel it in your body? People talk about not being able to speak when overwhelmed with sadness or grief because of «a lump in their throat» or a heaviness in their chest or body. How are you physically experiencing your sadness and grief? Sit and breathe, and notice how you respond to a memory when you felt very sad. This isn't a question about what you are thinking but what you are physically feeling in your body—the sensations of tightness and restriction in your body. For each negative emotion, you can document a list of physical sensations linked to experiencing that emotion.

This tool connects us to what we are feeling in our bodies. In this way we can fully experience our emotions. We can sit with them by noticing their physical sensations and not feel overwhelmed by them. By sitting and feeling these sensations, we allow our emotions to fully express themselves. As soon as our emotions are expressed, the sensations linked to them diminish and leave. You don't need to know the name of the

Drink From the Well

emotions to release it this way. All you need to be able to do is to feel the sensations in your body.

This tool is called "Surfing Our Emotions" for two reasons. The first is that like the water in the ocean, our emotions also move in waves. They begin, they build in intensity, they peak, and then subside and disappear. The second is that rather than being surrounded by water and perhaps feeling like you might drown, as a surfer you are standing on your surfboard riding the wave of water. You are only interacting with the water via your surfboard. When we surf our emotions, we too are riding on top of the wave of emotion rather sitting in the middle of it. We also are only engaging with the emotion, via the physical sensations associated with it and not surrounded by and drowning in both the mental and physical aspects of it.

When we "surf" our emotions, we are choosing to feel our negative emotions, to acknowledge and accept them, and allow them to be expressed. As a result, like waves, they simply subside and disappear. We can release our fears. We can move on with our life without carrying our negative emotions with us. We can learn to become physically aware of our emotions, before we consciously recognize we are feeling them.

Emotions create waves of all sizes depending on how strongly we feel them. Some of our emotions are large and take time to "surf". Others are small and take only a few seconds. When we start to "surf" an emotion, we have no idea how big or small it is. Only when we begin to surf it will we get a sense of

Eliora

its size. You will know how big an emotion is by how quickly it builds in intensity and ebbs away. With surfing, it doesn't matter how large the wave is because we are always sitting on top of it. This means we don't have to worry about the size and intensity of the emotion we are surfing or about being overwhelmed. When we surf, we are detached and peaceful as we ride the wave of the sensation linked to the emotion until it disappears and the emotion is gone.

The only time we can actually surf our emotions is when they are moving like waves through us. The moment we get attached to the emotions because we believe we need to feel them to make sense of them or our lives, that is when they stop passing through us as a wave. When we repeat the stories in which these emotions occurred, the emotions become even more intense and we become more attached to them. So rather than the emotion moving in a wave that peaks and disappears, when we relive our stories, the emotions get bigger, stronger and we become attached to them. This tool "Surfing your emotions" helps us avoid reliving of our stories, by inviting us to focus on our exhale so that our "thinking" mind is too busy watching the sensations of breathing out to actively think.

Tools to Connect: **Surfing Your Emotions**

1. Focus on your exhale. The sound of the air leaving your body, and the feeling of the air passing out of your chest as it moves inward and down. Focus on breathing out, just sit and notice your breath. This is the starting place so that we can let go of thinking and check in with what we are feeling inside our body.

2. As you focus on breathing out, your thinking mind is kept busy. This allows you to be present in the moment, to let go, to drop down, and relax into your body.

3. Once you are settled into your body, scan your body for any sensations linked to emotions. These sensations tend to feel like tightness and restriction. They can occur anywhere in your body and come and go as you experience your emotions. There are four places they tend to occur: in the jaw, throat, chest, and stomach.

- **The Jaw.** Notice any clenching and tightness in your jaw. Try opening and closing your mouth and notice any restriction.

- **The Throat.** Notice any difficulties swallowing, a lump in your throat, and/or general tightness in the muscles surrounding the throat.

- **The Chest.** Notice any heaviness your chest. Take a deep breath in and notice if your chest feels especially tight.

- **The Stomach.** Notice any sensations of queasiness, churning, butterflies, or a sinking feeling in your stomach.
- Scan and feel for tightness in other areas of your body as well. These sensations tend to come and go as your emotions are triggered within you. For some people, who express specific negative emotions almost all the time, the associated sensation will feel like it's constantly there.

4. It's normal to feel multiple emotions at one time, so you may feel tightness and restrictions in several areas of your body. Since you can only "surf" one emotion at a time, you must choose one sensation to sit with and observe. It doesn't matter which one, you can come back and "surf" any of the other emotions you are sensing later.

5. Once you have chosen the sensation you want to "surf," the next step is to return to focusing on your exhale. By focusing on your exhale, you are letting go of thinking and instead connecting with your body and the sensations you are feeling there. You are also keeping your conscious mind busy so you don't get caught up in reliving the memory.

6. Continue to focus on your exhale, and when you feel relaxed, begin to keep an eye on the sensation you have chosen to surf. Ninety percent of your focus will be on your exhale and ten percent will be on watching the sensation. The easiest way to do this is to notice where on the wave you are with respect to

this sensation. Is it still increasing in intensity, is it peaking and beginning to subside, or is it gone all together?

7. As you "surf," you are creating time and space to sit with your emotions by observing their sensations. If you find yourself thinking, gently bring your focus back to your exhale and the sensation you are surfing.

8. As you watch this sensation you will ride the wave until it finally goes away. Once it has disappeared, you know this specific emotion has been fully expressed and released.

9. Some emotions are very intense and come in as tsunami-sized waves and others are as small as ripples. The size of the wave determines how long it will take to complete the "surf." The larger the wave, the longer it takes before it peaks and recedes. You cannot make the process go faster or slower. You are merely watching the wave, not exerting control.

10. Each emotion you "surf" and release is now no longer attached to you. This doesn't mean you won't feel similar emotions associated with that particular situation or in future situations. However, that one emotion you surfed, which is associated with a particular aspect of the situation, is gone and you are free of it forever. You can remember that moment and the emotion will no longer be felt.

The Five Basic Steps to Surfing.

1. Scan your body for sensations associated with your emotions.

2. If you are experiencing more than one sensation, choose just one that you will "surf."

3. Focus on your exhale.

4. Continue focusing on your exhale and start to observe the sensation you have chosen to 'surf' Ninety percent of your focus will be on your exhale, and ten percent on the sensation.

5. Once the sensation is no longer felt, you have finished surfing that emotion and it has been released.

Quiet

My mother needs me to be quiet.

"She's an introvert," she explains. "She needs quiet."

Like my sister, who is quiet. She takes naps. Lies on her stomach in the sun by the window for hours like a cat.

My mother needs me to be quiet.

To be less.

To not make noise.

Not take up space.

Not threaten her sanity.

My mother wants, needs, and expects me to be invisible.

Especially when she is tired, she needs me to disappear into my room like a vapor.

Like the ghosts in the stories, I read late at night when I am supposed to be sleeping.

Fear Is the Basis for All Destructive Actions and Behaviors

Fear →	Primary Emotions →	Secondary Emotions →	Destructive Behaviors
	Such as: Hurt	Such As: Anger	Such As: Rejecting
	Disappointed	Rage	Being Dismissive
	Rejected	Hate	Ridiculing
	Used	Bitterness	Shutting Down
	Hopeless	Resentment	Seeing only the Bad
	Unloved	Frustration	Overeating
	...	...	...

When we are filled with negative emotions—especially the powerful, destructive Secondary Emotions of hate, anger, rage, resentment, and bitterness—we often feel we have no choice but to unleash these emotions on ourselves, other people, or the world. Our Secondary Emotions have a destructive quality that pushes us to hurt, cause pain, and punish ourselves and others. We do this by blaming and shaming; attacking verbally, emotionally, and physically; dismissing, demeaning; disrespecting; undermining; gaslighting, etc. Our fear is the source of our negative emotions and destructive and hurtful behavior towards ourselves and others. As a result of our fear, we ultimately create even more Darkness in ourselves and those around us.

The Role of Distractions

When we are afraid, we look to distractions to decrease the intensity of our negative emotions and to help us ignore how uncomfortable they make us feel. We use them to distract ourselves from thinking about the problem, the source of our fear and negative feelings, by focusing our attention on something we "enjoy" that keeps our mind busy. Depending on the distraction and the moment this "enjoying" can be either emotionally, mentally, and physically pleasurable or destructive.

Three types of distractions include:

1. **Substances** – Some substances we use for distraction dull our emotions or our senses, sending us into a stupor. Other substances create new sensations and emotions within us that divert us from our current emotional angst. We take these substances into our bodies in the belief they will help us cope with our fears and negative emotions. This includes such substances as alcohol, tobacco, food, especially sugar, drugs such as cannabis, kava, and opioids, chemical compounds such as airplane glue. In that moment we may feel free of the torment of our emotions and our lives, such as feeling lost, angry, hurt, alone, purposeless, rejected, and worthless. Unfortunately, once these substances have left our system, the emotions we hoped to escape are still there waiting for us.

2. **Activities** – We all have specific activities we do to distract our minds from our current problems and pain. These activities

makes us "feel" good and help distract ourselves from feeling emotions such as agitated, upset, down, alone, or afraid. When we are playing virtual games, shopping, gambling, scrolling through social media, etc., our minds are engaged in two different ways. First, we become so focused on the activity that we lose connection to the present and second, the activity is so engaging we want to continue doing the activity. The problem comes when we don't want to or cannot stop.

3. **Stories** Often when we are overwhelmed with life and negative emotions, stories help us distract ourselves from what we are feeling. These stories aren't the childhood tales like Jack in the Beanstalk or Hansel and Gretel. These are our personal stories that we tell ourselves repeatedly to help distract us from our emotions, especially our fear. When we tell ourselves a story, the words of the story create a familiar path we walk down again and again. The words and the sentiments behind the words are familiar, they are part of who we tell ourselves we are. They create a soothing sensation in our minds. For example, we may tell ourselves the story "No one loves me." Those 4 words take on a power of their own when we repeat them over and over again in our minds. Like the sound of a train moving down the tracks—a clickity clack, sound that relaxes our bodies. Other examples of stories include "No one appreciates me," "I am the best," or "I work harder than everyone else" It matters less the actual meaning of the word than the importance of the

sentiment to our sense of self and the feeling repeating those words has on how we feel inside.

Our distractions are a type behavior that are triggered when we feel fear and other negative emotions. Because it is fear driven, there is always some level of destructiveness involved. This is because we are choosing to run away from our fears and negative emotions rather than dealing with them directly, so that we can be free of them.

Fear Is Only Overwhelming and Controlling When It is Repressed

When fear is repressed and ignored, it can become overwhelmingly powerful and scary. It becomes like a dark monster hidden in our closet, waiting to destroy us. We hide from it, believing it's safer not to look or know in case it's even bigger, more powerful and destructive than we think it is. Only when we turn on the lights can we see that the fear is tiny and nothing in comparison to the monster we feared. When we see our fears for what they are, we realize they are not in the least scary.

A Daughter's Gifts

You know the story. The princess is born, and the Queen invites the fairies to bestow gifts upon her precious new child. Except this happened recently, and the fairies had disappeared, fading into the green hills long before the Queen came along. No matter, she would perform the ritual in the fairies' place by imagining the gifts they'd grace her child with and then blessing the baby girl herself.

She carried her daughter through the pine needles into the forest, into the clearing with the milk-white light and fireflies. She laid her child on the nest of needles, lit a candle, said a prayer, and cast her blessings over her daughter's tiny face.

"My daughter, I bless you with a small voice. If no one hears you, they'll never criticize you for what you say. Second, I gift you mediocrity so you will never cause jealousy in men or women. Third, I bless you with the most modest of dreams. If you never extend yourself far, you'll never experience the pain of failure. Fourth, I bless you with the absence of desire. If you desire nothing, you will never be disappointed. Fifth, I gift you the power of invisibility. If no one sees you, they'll never be able to hurt you, ostracize you, or kill you."

The Queen gazed down at her sleeping babe, and blew out the candle with satisfaction Now, she knew her daughter would be protected against everything.

The Cascade of Darkness That Follows Fear

Our fear amplifies when we get caught up in our Darkness or the Darkness of others. It is like a downward spiral that can take us further and further in to negativity, insecurity, and fear. As we become more filled with Darkness, our interactions with others become more disappointing and unforgivable, as we focus our attention on what's wrong or bad in them, in ourselves, in the relationship. We enter into a self-perpetuating cycle of having expectations and not having them met, and of responding to the fears of others with more fear.

What happens to any of us when we feel fear? We know that it triggers a cascade of Dark emotions and behaviors. It activates specific subconscious beliefs that were created or adopted to help us cope with this fear. These beliefs immediately begin to affect our perspective, skewing our understanding of reality so we only see those aspects that confirm these beliefs. We then begin to respond to the fear as our patterns associated with these beliefs directs us.

When we feel fear, it is often the negative emotions and the destructive behaviors that they trigger that we notice first. They have a profound effect on our lives. How many of us base our decisions on our mood? We fail to understand these moods wouldn't be there at all without the initial fear.

Let's look at a day in the life of someone who is experiencing fear. Imagine Sam has applied for a job and has learned that they were turned down. A number of fears are being triggered in Sam as soon as they receive the news. Immediately they fear they didn't get the job because we the company thought they were useless and worthless because they didn't have the right type of experience for that particular job. They also fear now they have been turned down that they won't get the financial security, and recognition for their skills that they think they want and need. Lastly they are afraid that because they failed to get the job that some of their friends may judge them and perhaps even reject them.

From these fears, Sam now starts to feel embarrassed and ashamed that they were rejected. They feel hopeless and discouraged about a getting a job. As Sam struggle to cope with the disappointment of not getting the job, there is a very good chance they are not recognizing each of the primary emotions they have been feeling. As a result, their secondary emotions are now being triggered as they start to feel resentful that the company has treated them this way. They are angry and bitter that others have jobs when they cannot get one. As their feelings of anger, resentment, and hate build, they begin to lash out at their friends who have jobs and can afford the good things in life that Sam longs to have. They lash out at family members who are trying to be understanding and supportive.

Drink From the Well

At the same time as all these Dark emotions and behaviors are occurring, specific subconscious beliefs are starting to taking control of Sam's perspectives, thoughts, and behavior. The subconscious beliefs that have been triggered in Sam include "To be safe, I must always be the best," and "To be safe, I must never be held responsible for any mistakes or failures." As these beliefs begin to skew Sam's take on reality, they are beginning to find reasons why it was the company's fault, the interviewer's fault, their partner who suggested they wear green's fault, they didn't get the job. The more Sam thinks about it the more they are convinced that the interviewer didn't know their stuff and had no idea what they were doing. Sam's mind begins to focus on all the ways they were superior to the interviewer, especially in appearance. This leaves Sam feeling safe, knowing they are better than the person who interviewed them.

As Sam continues focusing on his mistreatment at the hands of this interviewer who is to blame for his rejection, he feels that life, and the world are against him. How can he possibly succeed with people like the interviewer out in the world, who don't appreciate his skills and abilities. Feeling angrier and more abused and resentful with every rehashing of the rejection story, Sam is become so reactive that people start to avoid him. What started as not getting a job has turned into a downward spiral of Darkness in which Sam is overwhelmed with negative emotions and destructive behaviors and patterns which they direct at friends and family that happen to get in the way. Sam, now filled with Darkness is spreading Darkness to everyone he knows.

Our Dark responses to fear are avoidable. As we learn to see and acknowledge the fear that is the root of our painful, hurtful feelings, and responses, we no longer feel them or need to act on them.

Attack Reject Hurt Undermine Demean Punish

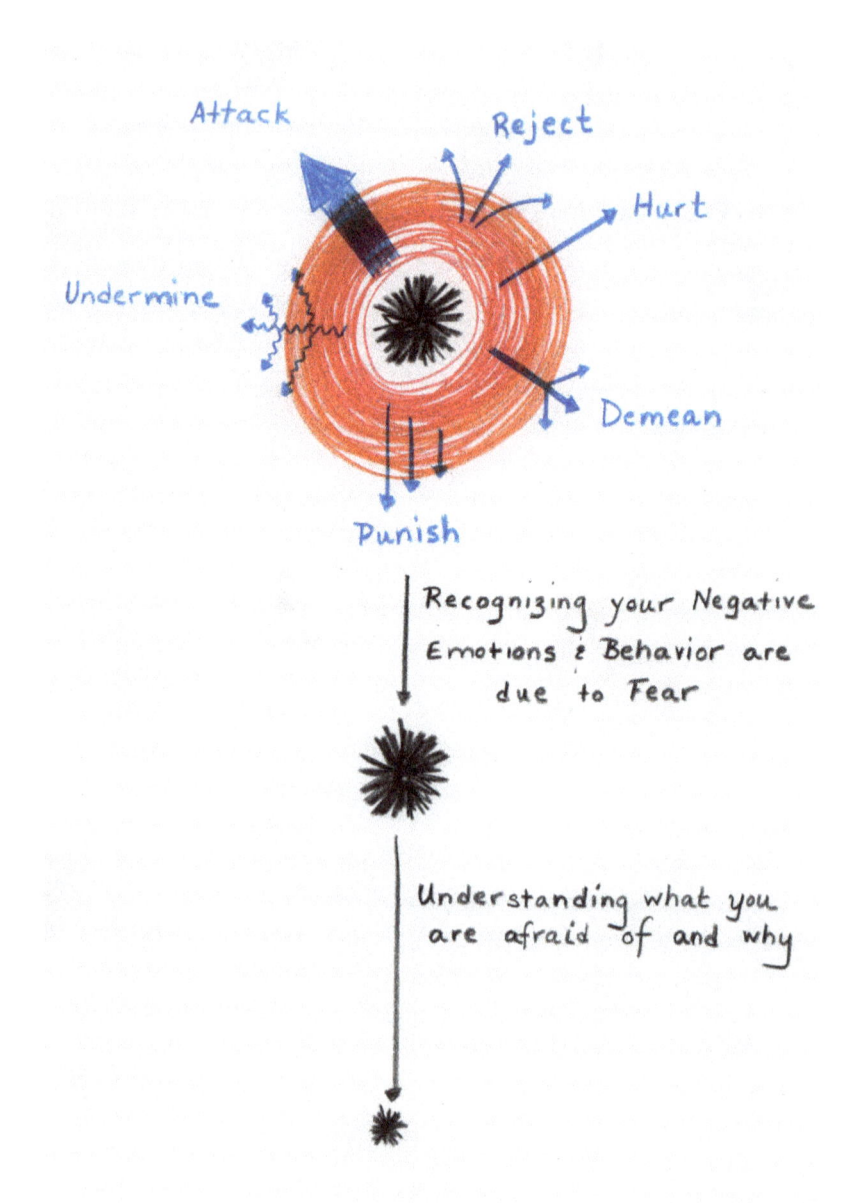

Recognizing your Negative Emotions & Behavior are due to Fear

Understanding what you are afraid of and why

Eliora

Tools to Connect: **Connecting With Your Fears**

When you use this tool, you will be freed of the tyranny of your own fears controlling your emotions, behavior, perspective, and thoughts. For the first time in your life, you will be able to control your fear rather than letting it control you. The basis for this tool is the recognition of fear being the trigger for all the Darkness that follows it. When our minds make the connection between our Darkness and fear, we no longer need to express the Darkness. It's as if we are only expressing this Darkness to bring attention to the fact we are feeling fear.

The first step to using this tool is noticing you are feeling negative emotions, engaging in destructive and hurtful behaviors, and caught up in negative patterns. The second step is to recognize that these negative feelings, behaviors, and patterns are the result of feeling fear. When you recognize and accept that whatever negative state, you are in is the result of fear, then the negative emotions, behaviors, thoughts, and patterns no longer need to be expressed. As a result, they lessen in intensity and disappear. The final step is understanding what fears are responsible for this response. By looking objectively at our fears, they lose their power and you can see them for the small, slightly pathetic emotions they are. As they lose their power, they also lose their ability to control you by negatively affecting your thoughts, perspective, feelings, behaviors, and patterns.

The Steps in Connecting with Your Fears

1. The first step is noticing you are feeling negative emotions, and/or you are hurting yourself, or other people. Often the easiest way to determine if you are feeling these Dark emotions is to check in and notice what you are feeling in your body. When we feel agitated and very tense, it's most often because we are feeling strong negative emotions.

2. The next step is to create a list of how your fear is negatively affecting you at that moment. Notice your emotions, the ones you are aware of consciously and those you feel in your body. Notice how you are behaving in hurtful ways to yourself or others. Notice your fantasies about how you would like to hurt yourself and others. Lastly, notice if you are caught up in one of your patterns.

This noticing includes:

- Any emotions you are feeling. This includes any of our negative emotions: anger, sad, hurt, resentment, frustrated, hate, depressed, unloved, etc. It also includes any sensations of tightness or restriction you are feeling in your body, such as a clenched jaw, a heavy chest, or queasy stomach.

- Any ways you are behaving or fantasizing about behaving that hurt yourself or others. This includes such behaviors as: ignoring someone who is trying to explain something to you, spending more money than you can afford, lashing out at others, catastrophizing, shutting down and pushing others away, comparing yourself to others and feeling either better than them and putting them down, or feeling worthless compared to them and putting yourself down. These destructive behaviors also include any distractive behavior that feels compulsive and is hurting you.

- Any patterns that are controlling you. This includes any of the blaming patterns: "Blaming-In," "Blaming-Out," "Pretending." It includes all the patterns that protect you from feeling or appearing worthless and defective including "The Best of the Best," "Wallflower," "Mr. or Ms. Right," or "Fake It 'til You Make It."

3. Now it's time to identify your fears. There are three questions to ask yourself about why you are afraid. Depending on the situation, sometimes all three questions will be relevant and sometimes just one or two. Be as specific as you can in the answers.

1st Fear: What are you afraid is wrong with you that is causing this problem or situation?

Imagine being back in the situation when you got upset (i.e. when the fear was triggered). What are you telling yourself are the reasons it's your fault? What are you seeing that is wrong in you that is the cause for the situation? What are you afraid others will think of you or how they will judge you that is linked to this situation?

Example: I did poorly on an assignment. Now I'm afraid my teacher or boss will think it's because I'm stupid, incapable, and incompetent.

Example: I'm the only person in my group that wasn't invited to the party. I'm afraid it's because no one likes me or wants to be with me.

2nd **Fear: What are you afraid you won't get in this situation that you think you want and need?**

Imagine being back in the situation when you got upset (i.e. when the fear was triggered). What are you convinced you need and want that you are now afraid won't happen or you won't get now?

Some answers are more specific like a clean house, a day off, or a partner that listens to you and pays attention to you. Some answers are more general like power, success, love, or fun.

Example: All I do is work, work, work. I work all the time at my job and at home. I'm so afraid I'll never get a chance to just relax, have some fun, and spend time with friends.

Example: I just spent hours cleaning out the basement for a friend and I promised another friend to help them as well. I'm so afraid if I don't help others out and constantly give, no one will like me, appreciate me, or want to be with me.

3rd Fear: What are you afraid you will lose either from your life or from who you are?

Imagine being back in the situation when you got upset (i.e. when the fear was triggered). What aspects of your life are you afraid are being threatened with change? What aspects are you afraid you will lose?

External Losses—losing something external to you like a friendship, money, a promotion, or belonging to a group.

Example: I have a great group of co-workers that I really enjoy hanging out with and now that I just got promoted, I'm afraid my new position will change the way they see me and how comfortable they are with me. I'm afraid I won't belong to the group anymore and they won't include me.

Imagine being back in the situation when you got upset (i.e. when the fear was triggered). What aspects of—who you are, how you respond to people, how you see yourself, how others see you- are you afraid will change and that you will lose?

Internal losses—losing something within you such as a role that you play like a caretaker, the boss, or perhaps even losing seeing yourself as a failure if you were finally to succeed.

Example: My last child just moved out and is living on their own. I don't know who I am and what I should be doing with my life now that I no longer playing the role of Mom because my kids are all grown up.

4. You will know you have identified exactly the right fear, when as you think about a fear, your body gives a sigh of relief and relaxes. Listen to your body; it will let you know whether your answers are correct or not. Note down any of the answers that resonated with you.

5. There are three sentences to say out loud to yourself. This process of reading the sentence, saying, and hearing it, helps you take in their message. Don't skip or adlib any of the sentences. With these three sentences you are recognizing that you are feeling fear, it is taking over, and it is causing a Dark reaction with specific negative emotions, behaviors, and patterns. By realizing fear is present and is responsible for these Dark responses, you now no longer need to express them and they simply disappear and leave you feeling only the fear. By identifying and then acknowledging the actual fears responsible for this reaction, the fears become less overwhelming and they lose their power to control you and subside into nothingness.

Now is the time to use the information you wrote in Step Two (the emotions, behaviors, and patterns you are expressing) and Step Three (your fears) to complete the third sentence.

(1) **This is me,** (*your name*), **filled with fear.**

(2) **This is me,** (*your name),* **overwhelmed with fear.**

(3) This is me, (*your name*), **expressing that fear right now by feeling** (the emotions you are feeling), **by doing** (the hurtful behaviors you are doing or fantasizing about doing), **by being caught up in my pattern of** …….. (*Blaming or Protection from Worthlessness*), **because I am afraid** (the fears you identified).

6. Take a breath and notice what you are feeling in your body. Is there a shift? Are your negative emotions becoming less intense? How strongly do you want to continue behaving in the ways you listed? Lastly, how caught up are you in your pattern(s)? Can you choose another way of responding?

7. Four possible ways you may be responding.

- You may feel more relaxed and at peace, less reactive and neutral, with less push or no push to behave in hurtful ways. If this is the case, you have successfully Connected with your Fears and you have released both the Darkness and the underlying fears.

- You may still feel reactive with exactly the same emotions and behaviors as when you started. In this case, it's a question of correctly identifying the feelings, behaviors, and patterns that are the most meaningful for you as you express this fear at this moment. Be as specific as you possibly can in your answers. It may be helpful to ask your Deepest Wisdom for answers, especially about the actual fears that underlie this response. Let the relief you feel in your body when you correctly identify the responses and fears be your guide.

- You may still feel reactive but with different emotions as compared to the last time you checked in. This is because there is another layer of emotion, behavior, patterns, and underlying fears that you will need to work through before you can let go of all the fear that was triggered in you in that moment. It's like peeling an onion, removing one layer at a time until there is no onion left. You will need to ask yourself what negative feelings am I experiencing now? What hurtful behaviors am I doing or fantasizing about doing now? What patterns am I caught up in now? What fears are present now? Expect a very different list of answers from the last time. Say your three sentences. Take a deep breath and check in. If you are still reactive, repeat these steps with each of the new layers that keep emerging as you removed the previous ones. Continue doing this until you are relaxed and at peace, neutral and feel no push to behave in hurtful ways.

- When you check in, you feel totally blocked. You can hear yourself saying, "No way, I'm not going to change". Any resistance you are feeling is because you are afraid. You are not alone. The next section is dedicated to explaining how to work through the fears that are causing resistance.

Resistance to Letting Go of Our Fear and Darkness

Through the course of our lives, fear and Darkness have always been in control. The familiarity and predictability of our Dark responses to fear makes us feel safe. As we work to let go of our Darkness by acknowledging our fears and the negative emotions, behaviors, and patterns they trigger, we sometimes feel afraid and resistant to changing the status quo. This is normal. For some of us, we are resistant to changing specific fears or responses. For others, there is push back to letting go of any part of their Dark response. Any resistance we are feeling is due to fear. By using the tool, 'connecting with our fear', we can let go of not only the fear but the resistance as well.

The best way to tell if you are feeling resistant is to notice any pushback or fear when you try to use the "Connecting With Your Fears" tool, or when you think of letting go of negative emotions or responses. If this is the case, you will need to use the tool Moving Through Resistance to address the particular fears that comes up when you think of releasing your Darkness.

Tools to Connect: Moving Through the Resistance

1. Take a few breaths, focusing on your exhale, allowing yourself to relax and feel safe. Now imagine letting go your Dark response to fear. Imagine letting go of the negative emotions, behaviors and patterns you are currently expressing. Now take a moment and notice what feelings you are experiencing in response and write them down. It could be an emotion you recognize at a conscious level like anger or sadness or an emotion you feel in your body like a clenched jaw or lump in your throat. Notice the ways you want to behave or are fantasizing about behaving. Add these to the list. Lastly, notice if you are feeling caught up in one of your patterns. Add these to list as well.

2. What are you afraid will happen if you let go of your Dark response? There are three common fears triggered in this particular situation. 1) There is something wrong with you and you need to respond with Darkness because it punishes you for being defective. 2) By changing, you will lose the relationships and people most important to you. 3) By changing, you will lose your sense of self.

> **1st Fear: There is something wrong with you and responding with Darkness punishes you for it.**
>
> *Imagine letting go of your fear and your response to it, so that you feel happier and lighter. What are you afraid you will be losing that you deserve to feel? How is the Darkness*

punishing you? Why do you need to be punished? What is wrong with you?

Example: I am so ugly, no one could possibly love me, including myself. I deserve to feel rejected and to be treated with contempt and unkindness by others and by myself as well.

Example: I am such a disappointment to my family that I deserve to be put down by them and then to further punish myself by hating and rejecting myself.

2nd **Fear: By changing, you will lose the people most important to you and your relationships with them.**

Imagine letting go of your fear and your response to it, so that you feel happier and lighter. Think about the important people in your life. Who are you afraid will be upset and maybe feel threatened if you were to change how much Darkness you felt? Who might be jealous if you felt happier than they do? Who might feel abandoned if they were down and unhappy and you don't join them in their Darkness and instead felt at peace and calm?

Example: I'm the person everyone in my family compares themselves to in order to feel more successful. I'm afraid if I am no longer controlled by my fear, I will stop saying no to growing, learning, and becoming more competent and capable. I'm afraid I might become more successful than they are and as a result they could no longer feel superior.

As a result, I'm afraid they would reject me and I would no longer belong.

Example: Whenever I get together with my friends, we spend the evening complaining and telling stories about what's going wrong in our lives. I'm afraid if I stop being in my Darkness and start focusing on what is good in my life rather than what is bad, my friends will feel unhappy about themselves and their lives and won't want to be with me anymore.

3rd Fear: By changing, you will lose your sense of self.

Imagine letting go of your fear and your response to that fear so you feel happier and lighter. What parts of yourself are you afraid you might lose if you were no longer filled with negative emotions like anxiety, inadequacy, or anger? What parts are you afraid you might lose if you were happier and loved and liked yourself?

Example: Everyone knows I can't control my temper and that when I get angry, I explode. I'm afraid if I was no longer controlled by fear, I wouldn't be angry. If this happens, I'm afraid I won't know who I am anymore and no one else would know either.

Example: I'm someone who is always anxious and afraid. It stops me from doing so many things I might like to do. I'm afraid that if I am no longer controlled by fear that I won't be able to use my anxiety as an excuse to hide and avoid any activity that is challenging. I'm afraid I will change so much that won't know who I am and how to be in the world anymore.

Ask yourself each set of question, focus on your exhale, and notice what answers are popping into your mind. Write them down. Pay attention to any feelings of relief as you identify your fears. This is the way your body lets you know that you have successfully recognized one of your fears.

3. Notice what exactly you are resistant to and write it down. Are you resistant to no longer feeling or being a specific way? Are you resistant to no longer being in your Dark in a specific situation? Or Are you resistant to no longer being in your Dark in general?

4. Use the information you listed in steps 2, 3, and 4 to fill in the third sentence. Say out loud to yourself.

(1) This is me, (*your name*), **filled with fear.**

(2) This is me, (*your name*), **overwhelmed with fear.**

(3) This is me, (*your name*), **expressing that fear right now by resisting letting go of my negative emotions, destructive behaviors, patterns, and thoughts I have in response to this situation** (*what is the situation you are resistant to changing how you respond?*) **and I am feeling** (*any emotions that I am feeling*) **doing** (*any hurtful behaviors you are doing or fantasizing about doing*), **by being caught up in my pattern of** .... (*Blaming or Protection from Worthlessness*), **because I am afraid of** (*what are your fears*).

Take another long deep breath in and out and see how you feel in your body now.

5. There are three possible ways you may be responding.

    - You may feel more relaxed and at peace, less reactive and neutral, with less push or no push to behave in hurtful ways. If this is the case, you have successfully Connected with your Fears and you have released both the resistance and the underlying fears.

    - You may still feel reactive with exactly the same emotions and behaviors as when you started. In this case, it's a question of correctly identifying the feelings, behaviors, and patterns that are the most meaningful for you as you express this fear at this moment. Be as specific as you possibly can in your answers. It may be helpful to ask your Deepest Wisdom for answers, especially about the actual fears that underlie this response. Let the relief you feel in your body when you correctly identify the responses and fears be your guide.

    - You may still feel reactive but with different emotions as compared to the last time you checked in. This is because there is another layer of emotion, behavior, patterns, and underlying fears that you will need to work through before you can let go of all the fear that was triggered in you in that moment. It's like peeling an onion, removing one layer at a time until there is no onion left. You will need to ask yourself what negative feelings am I experiencing now? What hurtful behaviors am I doing or fantasizing about doing now? What patterns am I caught up in now? Which fears are present now? Expect a different list of answers from the last time. Say your three sentences. Take a deep breath and check in. If you are still resistant, repeat these steps with each of the new layers that keep emerging as you removed the previous ones. Continue doing this until you are relaxed and at peace, no longer feel resistant to letting go of your Dark response.

6. Once you more at peace about changing how you respond to your fear with Darkness, then go back and retry making that first Connection with Your Fear.

Learning to Let Go of Our Fears

As we practice "Connecting to Our Fear," we actively recognize that our fear is responsible for our negative emotions, hurtful behaviors, and restrictive patterns. In doing so, we can release them because there is no longer any need to express them. An important part of "Connecting to Our Fear" is also understanding why we are feeling fear, to identify what we are afraid of, and why. For example, perhaps we are afraid to be open and vulnerable with the important people in our lives. As we sit and breathe, we check in with ourselves to identify exactly what the underlying fears are and if possible, why. We then discover that we are afraid that there is something wrong with us and as a result we are afraid we are unlovable and unlikeable. We are afraid no one could truly accept us and want to be with us. These are specific reasons why we are feeling afraid. When we identify our fears, we shine a light on them. As soon as we acknowledge our fears, they shrink from terrifying monsters to small, manageable, slightly pitiful fears. As soon as we look at them objectively for what they truly are and not what we fear they are, they lose their power over us to create and spread Darkness. We can be in the world in a new way, no longer controlled in that way by those fears.

In those moments when we can feel the fear but cannot identify it, we have another tool we can use, **Surfing Your Emotions**. When we surf our fears, we are connecting to the sensation the fear is creating in our bodies. In this way, we are slightly removed from the emotion, as if we are sitting on top it rather than drowning in the center of it. Now no matter how big or scary the fear feels, we will always feel safe "surfing" it: allowing it to be expressed, observing it pass through us as a wave and then disappear.

Darkness is Contagious

When people are afraid and filled with Darkness, it can spread quickly from one person to the next, as we react to their fear with our own. It's a bit like a virus. One person catches it and then before you know it, everyone they have been in contact with is contending with the virus and spreading it to all they meet.

There are three main reasons why Fear and its resulting Dark are so contagious. The first is because we rely on others to reassure us that we are safe, loved, and we belong. When they are caught up in Dark emotions, hurtful behaviors, and restrictive patterns, our subconscious and sometimes our conscious mind knows something is wrong. Sometimes we fear we are the problem and the cause of this upset. Sometimes we fear that there is a reason to be afraid which we aren't aware of yet. In these situations, any or all of the Ten Foundational Fears can possibly be triggered.

The second is that when others are filled with fear, they often express that fear with destructive and hurtful words and behaviors. When others lash out at us, put us down, abuse us, or push us away, we are flooded with an instantaneous and powerful response as fear is triggered in us. The bigger our fear response the more powerful the Dark cascade that follows and the more contagious our fear will be to others.

The last way we pick up on others' fears is when their Darkness results in our expectations not being met. Our expectations were created as protection from our most intense fears, so the moment one is not met, fear is instantly triggered in us. In this scenario, it adds another layer of fear to those already provoked by this person's Darkness.

As a result, fear and Darkness can spread from one person to the next, from one group to the next until the whole world seems to be afraid. But just as fear and Darkness can pass from person to person, so can our Light spread. For as we see the goodness and Light in ourselves, we are then able to see it in others, who can then see it in themselves.

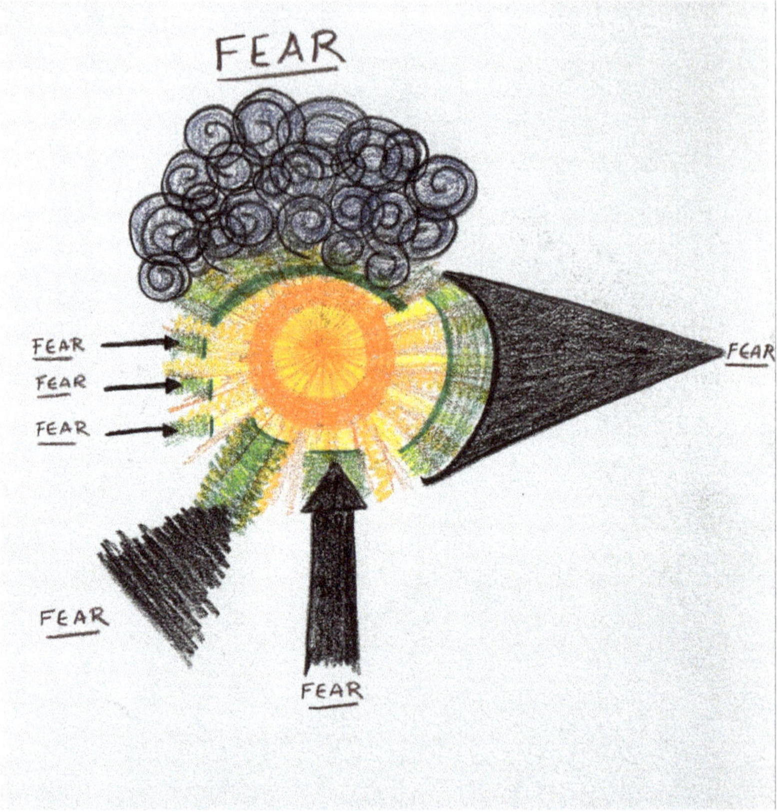
FEAR
FEAR
FEAR
FEAR
FEAR
FEAR
FEAR

Tools to Connect: **Creating a Light Shield**

When we are with anyone who is feeling fear, we have no choice but to pick up on it and respond with some fear and Darkness of our own. For example, imagine you are driving to work and someone beeps at you for being too slow as you move through a light. You might try to brush it off as nothing, but the fear and Darkness that was triggered in that moment is still with you. You are still feeling Foundational Fear #1. You are still feeling afraid you made a mistake, even a small one, and were judged and punished because of it. You are still expressing the negative emotions triggered by that fear: misjudged, mistreated, upset, unfairly punished. You may not choose to see it or feel it at a conscious level but it is there. If you were to take a minute and check in with your body, you would feel the sensations of tightness and restriction created from those negative emotions being expressed in you. An experience like this might not noticeably ruin your day, but it's still there, coloring your reaction and responses when other things go wrong, when other mistakes are made, and when other fears are triggered. It's partially filled you up with fear before your work day has even begun.

All day long we are responding to other people's fear with fear of our own. We've been doing this since we young. We've been allowing their fears to define us. We do this by letting their fears trigger fear in us which then colors our responses, our sense of self, and our choices. To make matters even worse, we don't know what to do with these fears and negative emotions and so we accumulate them, hundreds and thousands. Each fear and fear response adds strength and solidness to our Suit of Darkness, making it feel even more essential to our survival.

We have come to believe that taking on the fears of other is a necessary, unavoidable evil that is just part of life. We have learned we can still have moments to love, create, and feel joy and happiness despite it. But it's made our journeys through life so much harder, darker, and heavier than it has had to be. There is a tool available that in minutes will help you release anyone else's fear and Darkness, so that it is no longer there for you to carry through your day, your week, your life.

The first step in shielding ourselves from other people's fear and Darkness is noticing we are starting to feel negative emotions in response to their mood, words, or behavior. The second step is to accept that their fear and Darkness will negatively affect us no matter what we may think or decide to do about it. We may think that if we avoid spending time with them or perhaps if we decide we choose to not let it bother us, then we will be protected from their fear. It's true that it may help us avoid escalating the Darkness. But our need to do any of these things is us feeling afraid already before we have even interacted with them. By using this new tool, we will be able to see and accept that their hurtful behavior and bad mood are the result of their own fears. In this way, we can create a boundary in our mind with their fear and Darkness and thus avoid responding to it with fear of our own. We can let it be theirs and not ours.

The Steps to Create a Light Shield

1. Notice what you are feeling and how you are behaving in response to being with Person X. Has fear and darkness been triggered in you as a result of spending time with them? This could take the form of physically being with them, talking with them over the phone, texting with them, reading an email they wrote or a post they put up on social media, or even just thinking about them.

2. The next step is to notice what they are doing, saying, or feeling that is triggering fear in you. You will be need to come up with specific examples of the words they are saying, the way they are treating you, the emotions they are expressing that are hurting and upsetting you the most.

- Their expressed emotions could include any negative emotions: angry, sad, hurt, resentful, frustrated, hate, depressed, unloved, overwhelmed, jealous, etc.
- Their words, both said and unsaid, could include , "It's all your fault," "You are worthless," "You have it all wrong," or "I hate being with you," etc.
- Their behaviors could include attacking you, putting you down, shutting you out, blaming you, making you feel guilty, being passive aggressive, trying to control you, gaslighting you, etc.

- Their patterns could include any of the Blaming Patterns: "Blaming-In," "Blaming-Out," "Pretending," or the Protection from Being Judged as Worthless Patterns: "The Best of the Best," "Wallflower," "Mr. or Ms. Right," or "Fake It 'til You Make It."

3. Say these three sentences out loud. It's important that you not only think the sentences, but say them and hear them as well. *Don't skip any or adlib any sentence.* Each of these three sentences helps you recognize and accept that fear is present in Person X, it is controlling them, and they are expressing it with Dark emotions, behaviors, and patterns. By saying these three sentences, you also acknowledge these fears belong to Person X and not to you. In this way, you let Person X own their Darkness and don't take it on or make it your problem. Use the lists from Step Two to fill in the third sentence.

(1) **This is** (*Person X, and their role in your life*) **filled with fear.**

(2) **This is** (*Person X, and their role in your life*) **overwhelmed with fear.**

(3) **This is** (*Person X, and their role in your life*) **expressing their fears by feeling** (*any emotion they are expressing that is hurting you*), **by doing** (*any behaviors that are hurting you*), **by responding with the pattern** (*any pattern they are caught up in that is hurting you*), **and by saying** (*any words they are saying that are hurting you*).

4. After you say these three sentences aloud, take in a deep breath, exhale, and check in. Notice how you are feeling. How do you feel towards Person X now? How do you feel about being with them now? Are you still holding onto any anger or resentment towards them?

5. How do you feel about yourself now? Do you still feel hurt, mistreated, or perhaps disrespected? Are their negative emotions and behaviors still hurting you, upsetting you? Or do you feel relaxed and at peace with Person X and with yourself?

6. Four possible ways you may be responding.

- You may feel more relaxed and at peace, less reactive and punished by Person X's fears and Darkness. If this is the case, you have successfully created a Light Shield with Person X.

- You still may feel reactive with exactly the same emotions and behaviors. If so then, most likely you haven't pinpointed exactly what about Person's X Darkness causes it to feels so punishing and hurtful to you. The more specific you can be, the greater the sense of relief you will feel in your body when you identify it.

- You may still be reactive but with different feelings than before. This suggests that your interaction with Person X has multiple layers of fear and Darkness that need to peeled away one at a time like an onion until the whole of your fear response is gone. You will need to ask yourself what is Person X feeling now that is hurting me? Which of their behaviors are hurting and upsetting me now? Which of their patterns is upsetting me now? Expect a different list of answers from the last time. Say your three sentences. Take a deep breath and check in. If you are still reactive, repeat these steps with each of the new layers that keep emerging as you removed the previous ones. Continue doing this until you are relaxed and at peace, feel neutral towards Person X and their feelings, behaviors, and patterns.

- When you check in, you feel totally blocked. You can hear yourself saying, "No way, I'm not going to let go of my Dark response to Person X". Your resistance to changing this Dark interaction you are in with Person X is because you are afraid. The next section will explain how to work through the fears that are causing the resistance.

By not responding to Person X's Darkness with fear and negative emotions, you are not creating more Darkness as you feel anger, hate, and a need to hurt them. Instead, you are responding from a feeling of strength, peace, and clarity. This doesn't mean you are condoning their behavior or becoming a door mat. You have the ability now to create cleaner, clearer, and stronger boundaries with their hurtful behavior because their fears and your fears are no longer getting in your way.

Creating a Light Shield is a gift that you give yourself. By recognizing that the Darkness in others is due to their fears and not yours, you no longer take on their fears. As a result, you no longer take their behavior personally. Your Light Shield transforms your response to one of peace and safety rather than of fear and Darkness. You now have the perspective that those acting badly, unkindly, cruelly are doing so because they are overwhelmed with their own fear. This allows you to be at peace with the person whether they are in their Dark or their Light. It allows you to be independent from their Dark.

Resistance to Changing the Dark Dance We Do with Others

We all have relationships which seem stuck in the Dark, and that we resist bringing into the Light. We can tell we are resistant to changing our Dark interactions with someone by noticing how upset and angry we feel when we imagine Creating a Light Shield. This resistance could occur at the idea of creating this shield in general or just for specific people or situations. To move through it, we will need to connect with the underlying fears and the Darkness it triggers in us.

There are four possible reasons why we may feel resistant to the idea of creating Light Shields. The first is change can feel scary. Most people hesitate to lose the familiarity and comfort they experience from old ways of being. They fear that the unpredictability that change can bring into their life will make them feel afraid and unsafe.

The second reason is that for some people they believe the Darkness provides a necessary punishment to themselves or the other person. Some are afraid to release their Dark interaction because they feel they deserve to be treated badly and punished by the other person's Darkness.

Others resist letting go of this need to punish because they fear they are letting Person X off the hook by no longer responding to their Darkness with Darkness. They may also fear that by not responding with Darkness, Person X may feel as if their Dark behavior is being condoned.

Third, for some people they cannot imagine any other relationship with Person X than the Dark one they have right now. It is part of their story, the way they understand themselves, their lives, and their history. It helps them make sense of their interaction with Person X and themselves. They define who they are by their Darkness: their patterns, emotions, and behaviors. They fear that without their Dark responses, and relationship, they will not know who they are or how to live their lives.

Most people have the mistaken belief that the Dark is more powerful than Light and will ultimately destroy the Light or anyone who is living from it. They fear if they let go of their Darkness and are in the Light, they are setting themselves up for hurt and pain. Nothing could be further from the truth. When we are in our Dark, fear is in control of our thoughts, emotions, perspective, and behavior. We can't decide for ourselves the best way to respond, engage, feel, or think or act because fear has taken over.

Being in our Light does not mean we lie down for others to step all over us. It means we can choose how we want to act rather than just reacting from fears. This is the key: *When we are in our Light, we can act rather than react.* Thinking and choosing how we want to act opens the door to possibilities, to interacting in new ways that neither you nor the other person could have ever dreamt was possible. Being in your Light helps you to remain strong and clear headed in the presence of fear.

Tools to Connect: **Moving Through Resistance of Creating a Light Shield**

1. The first step is to close your eyes and imagine no longer responding with fear, negative emotions, hurtful behaviors, patterns, and words to Person X's fear and Darkness. Imagine their Darkness no longer triggers fear in you. Imagine walking away completely unaffected by their fear and the Darkness they are expressing towards you.

2. Now notice what you are feeling in your body, how much tightness and constriction you are feeling. Create a list of the negative emotions you experience as you contemplate changing your interactions with Person X. Some common emotions for people thinking of releasing their familiar Dark responses include resentful, deprived, nervous, anxious, terrified, punished, unloved, abandoned. Don't forget to include any sensations linked to emotions you may be feeling in your body as well. What hurtful behaviors are fantasizing about doing? What patterns are you getting caught up in as you imagine letting go of this Dark way of interacting?

3. What are you afraid will happen if you let go of your Dark response? There are three common fears triggered in this situation. 1) There is something wrong with you and you deserve to continue in this Dark interaction as punishment. 2) By changing, you will lose your story casting you as the innocent,

good person in this Dark interaction. 3) By changing, you will lose your sense of self.

1ˢᵗ Fear: There is something wrong with you and you should be punished.

Imagine letting go interacting with Person X from a place of fear and Darkness. Imagine no longer taking Person X's Dark behavior personally. How do you feel about no longer being a target for their anger, blame, hurtful words, and behavior? What is so wrong with you that you believe you deserve to continue to be punished with Dark emotions and behavior from Person X? What is so wrong with you that you believe you need to punish yourself with your own fear and Darkness?

Example: When I'm with my partner and they yell at me and tell me it's all my fault that they are upset, it is only right that I be punished by their hurtful words, rage, and destructive behavior.

Example: When I make a mistake and get it wrong, I deserve to be told how stupid, useless, and worthless I am. I need to further punish myself by putting myself down and not taking care of myself.

2ⁿᵈ Fear: By changing, you will lose your story casting you as the innocent, good person in this Dark interaction.

Imagine letting go interacting with Person X from a place of fear and Darkness. What is the story you tell yourself based on this interaction? How do you see yourself in this story? How do you see Person X in this story? What are you getting from Person X treating you this way, that you are afraid you will lose if this relationship changes?

Example: When my partner yells at me and puts me down, it just shows me what an unkind and cruel person they are. It allows me to see myself as a victim to their Darkness. (The more specific you are in your self-description and Person X, the more release you will get from the story.)

Example: How dare they treat me this way, they deserve to be punished and to get it back as good as they dish it out.

3rd Fear: By changing, you will lose your sense of self.

Imagine letting go interacting with Person X from a place of fear and Darkness. If you let go of your Dark response and see the other person feeling calm, peaceful, and unaffected, what aspects of yourself are you afraid you will lose? What aspect of the way you behave are you afraid you will lose? What excuses to act with Darkness are you afraid you will lose?

Example: When people are unkind to me, it gives me an excuse to let loose with all the anger and rage I've been holding onto inside of me. It lets me let off some of the pressure I have been building all week.

Example: I know my relationship with this person is hard for other people to understand. This is just the way we interact and we've made it work for us. I don't know who I would be if I no longer had this relationship with them.

Work your way through the questions. Listen to what you are telling yourself and write it down. You will know if the fears are correct when you feel your body relax and give a sigh of relief.

4. Use the lists in Steps Two and Three to fill in the third sentence. Now say aloud to yourself.

(1) This is me, *(your name)*, **filled with fear**

(2) This is me, *(your name)*, **overwhelmed with fear.**

(3) This is me, *(your name)*, **expressing that fear right now by resisting letting let go of my negative emotions, destructive behaviors, patterns, thoughts and stories that I have with and towards Person X because I am feeling** *(any emotions that I am feeling)* **doing** *(any hurtful behaviors you are doing or fantasizing about doing)*, **by being caught up in my pattern(s) of** …….. *(Blaming or Protection from Worthlessness)*, **because I am afraid of** *(What are your fears?)*.

5. Three possible ways you may be responding.

- You may feel more relaxed and at peace as you think about creating a Light Shield in general or with a specific person. If this is the case, you have connected with your fear and released your resistance.

- You may still feel reactive with exactly the same emotions and behaviors as when you started. Often, it's a question of correctly identifying the feelings, behaviors, and patterns that are the most meaningful for you as you express this fear at this moment. You may have to reconnect with your Deepest Wisdom to help you answer the questions about the actual fears that underlie this response. Let the relief you feel in your body when you correctly identify the responses and fears be your guide.

- You may still feel reactive but with different emotions as compared to the last time you checked in. This is because there is another layer of emotion, behavior, patterns, and underlying fears that you will need to work through before you can let go of all the fear that was triggered in you in that moment. It's like peeling an onion, removing one layer at a time until there is no onion left. You will need to ask yourself what negative feelings am I experiencing now? What hurtful behaviors am I doing or fantasizing about doing now? What patterns am I caught up in now? What fears are present now? Expect a very different list of answers from the last time. Say your three sentences. Take a deep breath and check in. If you are still reactive, repeat these steps with each of the new layers that keep emerging as you removed the previous ones. Continue doing this until you are relaxed and at peace and feel no resistance to creating a Light Shield.

6. Once you have released the resistance, go back and create your Light Shield.

Section 6:

Making Sense of It and Moving Forward

When and How to Release Your Fear and Darkness

With so many new tools, it can be helpful to review the ones designed to release your negative emotions, Dark behaviors, and patterns, and when to use them. There are three tools described that help you respond differently to fear and Darkness: Surfing Your Emotions, Connecting with Your Fears, and Creating a Light Shield.

You can release any negative emotion using "Surfing" (pg 134) including any fears. This approach is useful when you know there is a problem because you feel it in your body but don't understand why it is present or what it is triggering in you. It takes more time than the other tools, but there is a meditative quality to "Surfing" that often gives you time to relax, connect with your body and emotions. As you spend time surfing, you are also teaching yourself to recognize you are feeling negative emotions by noticing the sensations they create in your body. In this way, you are learning to be aware when fear is present and starting to take control.

The tool "Connect with your Fears" (pg 151) allows you to release both your fears and the Dark responses that come from those fears. When you use this tool, you will examine your dark responses by listing the all the ways you are reacting to fear at that moment. As you recognize your own negative emotions, behaviors, and patterns and attribute them to the presence of fear in you, they are released and disappear. You will also try to identify the actual fears that are responsible for your Dark response. By looking objectively at the fear, it loses its power to overwhelm and control you. If at any time you are unclear of your actual fears are, you can always use "Surfing" as a backup tool to clear them.

Lastly, if your negative emotional response is due to Darkness and fears in others, you can create a Light Shield (pg 171) between you and the other person. With this shield, you create a barrier between yourself and the fears and Dark response of the other person. In this way, you don't respond to their Darkness with fear because you aren't taking it personally. You can be interacting with someone who is angry and filled with rage and attacking and trying to hurt you and with the Light Shield in place, you see that their emotions and behavior are completely separate from you. You see they are the just the result of this person's fear. You are not responsible for it. It's theirs.

There are three different scenarios that can benefit from using these tools to clean up your negative emotional responses.

1. **Releasing the painful emotions associated with difficult memories.**

Every time you experience fear and the Darkness that follows, and you don't know how to deal with them, to release them, then you hold onto them. As a result, there are thousands of such moments stored in your subconscious. Some of these memories are especially heavy and painful. You can reconnect with the Darkness associated with it every time you relive that memory. These painful memories are exceptionally powerful and control how you see and define yourself, how you interact with people, and how you live your life.

With these three new tools you can work through each of these painful memories and release any fear or Darkness associated with them. In this way, when you relive the memory, the pain and hurt are gone and the memory has lost its ability to control you.

The first step is to choose a memory that feels like a painful burden because it continues to negatively affect you. When these memories include other people, then the pain you are experiencing is often due to their fear and Darkness. In which case, the first step is create a Light Shield for each of them. Close your eyes and focus on one person at a time as you relive the memory. What are they doing or saying, feeling, in that moment? Their Dark response that triggers fear in you can range from small seemingly innocuous emotions like sadness or loneliness to a full onslaught of rage and hate. Don't assume it has to be big to create a fear response in you. Once you have created a list of their emotions, behaviors, words, and patterns then create a Light Shield" for that person. Repeat this process for every person who is present within this memory and sometimes even those who are tangentially associated with it in some way. As you create your Light Shields, you are releasing the fear and Darkness of others that has been negatively affecting who you are since the memory occurred.

Once you have created Light Shields to release any fear and Darkness from others, check in with the memory for your own fears and Dark response. You can use "Connecting with Your Fears" to release your negative emotions, behaviors, and patterns. If you have insight as to what fears are present in you, then you can use this tool to clear the controlling fears as well. If you are unsure of your fears, then use "Surfing" to release the fears.

As you work to let go of the negative emotions, destructive behaviors, and patterns associated with these memories, they become more neutral and you can remember them without pain. You will then be able to move forward in your live without Darkness from the past holding you back and weighing you down.

2. Releasing the fears and Darkness from situations in the future.

You can use these tools proactively, by imagining being in situations you are already fearing. It could be giving a presentation, having a difficult conversation, or making a major life change. Start by imagining those moments. If it feels too overwhelming, break the moment down into bite-size chunks. You'll know which parts upset you the most by thinking of each step and checking in with your body and noticing feelings of tightness and restriction.

For example, if doing a group presentation fills you with fear, you could break it down into smaller steps. To illustrate: Step one: thinking about what you want to present. Step two: writing the presentation and practicing on your own. Step 3: waking up that morning knowing that today is the big day and leaving home. Step 4: waiting for the time of the presentation to finally arrive and walking into the room. Finally, Step 5: giving the presentation.

Once you identify an aspect of the future that fills you with fear then you will need to choose the best tool for the job. You could choose to "Surf" by relaxing into your body, focusing on your exhale, feeling the emotions as they are expressed in your body and letting go of each one, one at a time.

If your fear of a future event seems linked to specific people then use "Creating a Light Shield". Think of all the people who may play a role in the event because they will be there or because they are associated in your mind with the event. Imagine the situation playing out as if it was happening right now and imagine what you fear each person will do, say, or feel at that moment that will trigger fear in you. Repeat this process for each person. Check in by thinking of the event and noticing how you feel now after you have created your Light Shields.

Situations we dread are often scary because we already can feel the fear we are not up for the challenge. We fear that we don't have what it takes to succeed because we are incompetent, incapable, defective, lacking, worthless, or any of the adjectives associated with Foundational Fear #6. As we feel this fear, it immediately triggers our pattern created to protect us from it as well as negative emotions and hurtful behavior. To clear these fears, you will need to use the tool "Connect with Your Fears". This tool will first allow you to release the Dark response created from this fear. When you identify what you are afraid is broken, defective, or lacking in you then you can see your fear for what it is and release it. You can always rely on "surfing" to help you clear your fear as well.

By doing all the emotional work before the situation arises, you will be surprised at how relaxed and confident you feel once the future arrives and you are experiencing it.

3. Releasing your fears and their Darkness as they occur in your life.

It can be a challenge to be aware of your negative emotions as they are happening to you. Most of us are oblivious to their presence until they overwhelm us and we are beginning to behave in hurtful and destructive ways. As you practice checking in with your body and looking for sensations of tightness and restriction, you will often notice you are feeling negative emotions before you are consciously aware of them.

You have three choices of how to work through these emotions and the underlying fear that is causing them. First, you can continue focusing on the sensations the emotions are creating in your body, and to "surf" each emotion, one at a time. Second, you can create Light Shields with the people you have interacted with throughout the day. Often, it's not clear there is a direct link between your negative emotions and a specific person until you start to create a shield and recognize that Darkness they were expressing and how it negatively affected you. Sometimes, it can just take a one sentence text to fill you with fear.

Once you have identified a possible interaction that may have caused your fear, then close your eyes and relive the moment when you read their message, heard their voice, or spent time with them. What emotions, behaviors, words, patterns triggered you? You may want to check in with your body to notice when this negative response is occurring in you. Now create a Light Shield for each person who may have contributed to the Darkness you are feeling.

It may be that your negative response is the result of your own fears so that you will need to use the tool "Connecting with Your Fears". Notice how you are feeling, behaving, thinking about behaving at this moment in time. Notice what you are focusing on, what patterns you are caught up in, what distractions you feel compelled to continue, what stories you are telling yourself. You can release their control over you by recognizing they are all the result of your feeling fear. You can then release the fear by identifying it and using the tool "Connecting with your fears" or if you can't identify it using the tool "Surfing your emotions".

By clearing your fears and Darkness regularly, you are choosing not to let them negatively control your thoughts, choices, interactions, and life. Instead, you are choosing to keep your "emotional home" clean, Light, and bright

When and How to Connect with your Light

To connect with your Light, you have a choice of four tools: "A Meditation to Connect with Your Light", "Connecting with the Light in Children", "Reliving Past Moments of Light", and "Listening to the Quiet Voice Within".

"A Meditation to Connect to your Light" (pg 9) is a wonderful tool to use for five to ten minutes every day. As you practice using it to connect to your Light, you develop a trust and connection to the quiet peaceful core within you. You learn you can rely on this tool whenever you feel overwhelmed and need to find the love and peace deep within you. By focusing on your exhale and actively letting go of thinking and feeling, you are helping yourself see that you are not defined by them but by the peaceful core within in you. You can finally feel the peace, love, and belonging you have longed and need to experience to feel safe.

In those moments when you feel out of sorts and are struggling to remember that you even have a Light, you can use the tools: "Reliving Past Moments of Light" (pg 62) and "Connecting with the Light in Children" (pg 35) to help remind you what it feels like to be connected to your Light, living from your Light. Remembering those moments or looking at photos that captured it instantly sparks your Light within you. They remind you that even when you are afraid and in the Dark, that your Light is still there burning brightly. They remind you that you have value, that you are lovable, and that you are enough. All truths you tend to forget when living controlled by fear.

Lastly, when you are confused and feeling lost, you can be guided forward from a place of love and Light rather than fear and Darkness by connecting with "the Quiet Voice within" (pg 44). It can be hard to find your way when the only voice you listen to is coming from fear, insecurity, and ego. What if I fail? What if no one likes me? What if I don't have what it takes? When you focus on your exhale, you begin to drop down and in and connect with your Light, the source of your Deepest Wisdom. This is the part of you that believes you have value, you are lovable, and you are enough. Listening to the quiet voice of Deepest Wisdom which relies on self-love and acceptance to guide you puts you on different path from the one you have been walking, that has been controlled by fear. A path focused on living up to expectations, hiding from difficult situations, and relying on external validation to prove you have worth. Once on this new path guided by Deepest Wisdom, you will instead focus on finding and living your purpose, on loving and being loved, and on giving to and receiving from others, to life, and the world.

Hazel

At twenty-five Hazel married a beautiful man. He adored her and provided for her and asked only that she remain his adoring partner. One day, a friend taught Hazel how to see beyond Darkness to Light. When she closed her eyes and saw Light, the world swam in colors, she floated out of her body, and became a spray of stars in the Milky Way. She knew then that she had always been a star, was a star, and would return to her state of star-ness when she popped out of her physical body again at the end of her life. This new understanding filled Hazel with joy. She was happy to come back into her body when she finished and opened her eyes. She was excited to walk around being both a star and a woman. She shared the exciting star revelation with Frank, her husband. She said she could teach Frank how to see Light and he could float up into space and feel his star life too. Instead of being excited Frank's face cranked into a scowl. He didn't want to try. He thought the idea was dangerous. For example, Frank said, they'd always loved making pasta with beef on Tuesdays but now she craved skillet seared green beans and zucchini and cilantro from their garden. It's just food, Hazel said. It doesn't change anything about us. But that was not true. Her job and some of her friendships were no longer enough. She woke up at 4:00am and spent hours gazing at the still dark sky, winking and waving at her new tribe. She felt the light of the stars shooting down into her cells, her bones, the follicles of her hair. Frank felt the cold space next to him in the bed and growled. She asked for weeks, for months, tried to beg and bribe him to try. *I'll eat pasta again if you do,* she said. *We can make it from scratch—crack the egg in the pile of flour and knead it with our hands.* Finally, Frank reluctantly agreed. He closed his eyes and with her help, he saw Light, and he went with her to the stars, deep in the universe and then he understood. It was a piece of himself he had found. Then he and Hazel sat up at night together, waving at the stars, asking for answers.

Moving Forward and Choosing to Live Free of Fear

Doing this work daily creates opportunities for us to be in our Light as to let go of our fear and Darkness. This includes all forms of Darkness: the Darkness triggered in us at this moment, the Darkness from the past we are carrying with us, and the Darkness we fear for the future. With less Darkness and fear, we are no longer under the control of our subconscious beliefs which have the power to distort our understanding of reality and control us with their protective patterns.

As we live our lives, no longer controlled by fear, we spend less time responding to others, life, and the world with negative emotions and destructive behaviors. Instead, we see the good within ourselves and others, and respond to life with clarity and peacefulness. Everything shifts within us and those we interact with, as we learn to see our fears, let go of the resulting Darkness, and instead to connect with and live in our Light.

Many of us mistakenly believe that to survive in this world, we must meet Darkness with Darkness. Being in our Darkness we mistakenly believe will make us stronger and less vulnerable. We have been taught to believe succeeding at the expenses of others is somehow superior to treating others with fairness and compassion. Look at individuals in the news, who are admired for their power, wealth, and drive to succeed. Look at individuals we choose as leaders to guide us and our countries into the future. Look at individuals we admire and emulate who let the fear of not getting what they want justify stepping on and over anyone who does not serve them. It's no wonder we have gotten turned around and believe that Darkness is better, more powerful, and stronger than Light—but nothing could be further from the truth.

When we see and recognize our fears and release them then we are free of the negative emotions, destructive behaviors, and patterns that fear creates. We see ourselves, others, life, and the world with a clear and open mind which allows a greater understanding and wider perspective of reality. This then allows us to be open to finding new ways of thinking, problem solving, interacting with others, and being in the world.

Just as fear and Darkness can spread, Light can be passed from one person to the next. As we see the Light and connect to the Light within ourselves, our focus shifts and we can see the goodness and Light in others. We can appreciate their Light even when they are struggling with their Dark. As we begin to treat them with respect and kindness, they in turn begin to see the Light within themselves. Imagine one person lighting a candle, then turning to their right and left and lighting the candles of those nearby. In turn, those people light the candles of those near them, thus creating a wave of light spreading in all directions from that first lit candle. You have the tools to help you let go of fear and Darkness, and to connect with your Light. As you use them, remember this image and let it inspire you to spread your Light.

Butterflies

We think butterflies flit about for their own amusement, enjoying their paper wings, geometry in air. We don't understand they're trying to attract our attention, not that of the flowers.

If we slow our heartbeats, we might be quiet enough to let one alight on our shoulder, our nose tips, our hands. Then we'll hear something, in the cochlea of the ear, like the ocean through a shell, the music we need to hear.

Music as food. The song of our destiny. The song of our soul.

www.ingramcontent.com/pod-product-compliance
Lightning Source LLC
Chambersburg PA
CBHW042008030325
22853CB00048B/481